# Jean Alesi

*Red Missiles*

**Many Thanks**

The authors would like to offer thanks to all who have helped in the production of this book. First and foremost, a special thanks to Jean Alesi, who gave of his time and energy in providing us with the information necessary to write our text. A big thanks to Alain Prost, who kindly accepted to contribute the foreword of our book. Thank you to Eddie Jordan and Ken Tyrrell, who voluntarily provided us with their quotes.

**Photographic Credit**

All photos belong to Dominique Leroy, except for: pages 17, 22 and 23 (Alain Patrice); 117 and 120 (Steve Domenjoz); 121 (Thierry Gromik).

---

ISBN 2-940125-09-0 (published in French under the title «Jean Alesi, trajectoires en rouge», ISBN 2-940125-08-2). Chronosports, Route de Denges 28B, CH-1027 Lonay, Switzerland. Tél. (++41 21) 803 31 15. Fax (++41 21) 803 31 16. Photoengraving by DPI, Gland, Switzerland. Printed in Italy by Sfera International / Garzanti Verga, Milano.

# JEAN ALESI
## *Red Missiles*

**Photography**
Dominique Leroy

**Texts and graphic design**
Luc Domenjoz

**Translated by**
Mara Hlasek

| | | |
|---|---|---|
| Chapter 1 | The Roots of Passion | 9 |
| Chapter 2 | Formula 3000 Champion | 13 |
| Chapter 3 | Formula 1 with Uncle Ken | 33 |
| Chapter 4 | The Move to Ferrari | 39 |
| Chapter 5 | First Red Missiles | 43 |
| Chapter 6 | 1992, to the Depths of Hell | 65 |
| Chapter 7 | 1993, the Slow Recovery | 67 |
| Chapter 8 | 1994, Hope's Coming | 69 |
| Chapter 9 | A Classic Day in Montreal | 105 |
| Chapter 10 | Geneva, a Peaceful Pitstop | 109 |
| Chapter 11 | From Red to a Rainbow | 111 |

CHRONOSPORTS
ÉDITEUR

*Dear Jean,*

*They've asked me to write the preface for a book dedicated to your life and career. It's a touchy assignment, but I take pleasure in doing it. It's my chance to say what an engaging character you are.*

*I can't talk about you without first drawing attention to the particularities of your personality, as it's hard to get to know you. You must admit, you're most well known on the Formula 1 circuit for your fiery temper. More and more, Formula 1 drivers are expected to be very calm, thoughtful and think before they speak about what's bothering them – but you're the most impulsive driver I know.*

*If, from time to time, you show your true colors for the camera crews, amongst the team, it's a hundred times worse. One day, you're the nicest guy in the world, the next day you're throwing your helmet against the wall of the motor home. One day you're wallowing in misery; the next day, you're the happiest man on earth.*

*This is what makes you special, this is part of your charm. To succeed in Formula 1, you've got to be charming: to convince a certain engineer, to acquire a certain privilege. The people around you fall under the charm of your personality; such a character is nearly old-fashioned in the aseptic world of modern Formula 1.*

# *Foreword*

*I most appreciated you as a teammate during the 1991 season. During the entire year we spent together, you struck me as so fragile, despite outward appearances. I wanted so much to protect you from the problems that face a Ferrari driver.*

*You're well aware of the fact that at Ferrari, they are masters of pitting their drivers against each other--they think that this will work to their advantage! This didn't work with you. We've remained very loyal to each other during the last season. It's great to see how we stuck together in the face of adversity.*

*You've been an ideal teammate during the time we've worked together. We've had a lot of fun outside the finals. The amusement sometimes went as far as the trials. Do you remember our little game? You made so much fun of my nose that each time I was in front of you in the qualies, I'd show it to you by lowering the car. It was harmless, but it made us laugh, and lightened the atmosphere.*

*Since this time, you've lived through a lot with Ferrari. It has made me happy to try to give you direction in your career choices, knowing all the while that you are not one to follow directions. You listen intently, then do whatever you already had in mind. By impulse, you are capable of your best and your worst. But I can only hope that you stay like this, because, once again, this is part of your charm...*

Alain Prost

First and Last names: *Alesi, Jean*
Date of Birth: *June 11, 1964*
Place of Birth: *Montfavet, France; near Avignon (Vaucluse Dept.)*
Residence: *Geneva, Switzerland*
Civil Standing: *divorced*
Children: *one girl (Charlotte)*
Hobbies: *skiing and tennis*
Favorite meal: *pasta*
Height: *170 centimeters*
Weight: *73 kilos*

**Professional career :**

First competition in 1981

1981: Go-karts. Vice-champion of the Blue Class "Provence Alps Cote d'Azur" League.

1982: Go-karts. Champion of the Blue Class "Provence Alps Cote d'Azur" League.

1983: Coupe Renault 5 Alpine Turbo – one win.

1984: Formula Renault.

1985: Formula Renault – 5th place in the Championship.

1986: Formula 3. French vice-champion with Dallara-Alfa-Romeo – two wins.

1987: Formula 3. French Champion with the Oreca team--seven wins and five pole-positions.

# *Curriculum Vitæ Jean Alesi*

1988: Formula 3000 with the Oreca team – tenth place in championships.

1989: Intercontinental Formula 3000 Champion with the team from Eddie Jordan Racing.

Formula 1 with Tyrrell's crew – two fourth places.

1990: Formula 1 with Tyrrell's crew – 9th in the championship with 13 points: two seconds places in the American Grand Prix in Phoenix and Montreal.

1991: Formula 1 with the Ferrari team – 7th in the championship with 21 points: three third places in the Grand Prix in Monaco, Germany (Hockenheim) and Portugal (Estoril).

1992: Formula 1 with the Ferrari team – 7th in the championship with 18 points: Two third places At the Grand Prix in Spain (Barcelona) and Canada (Montreal).

1993: Formula 1 with the Ferrari team – 6th in the championship with 16 points: one second place in the Italian Grand Prix (Monza) and a third place in the Grand Prix in Monaco.

1994: Formula 1 with the Ferrari team – 5th in the championship with 24 points: a second place in the English Grand Prix (Silverstone) and three third places in the Brazilian (Interlagos), Canadian (Montreal), and Japanese Grand Prix (Suzuka).

1995: Formula 1 with the Ferrari team – 5th in the championship with 42 points: one win in the Canadian Grand Prix (Montreal), and four second places at the Argentinean (Buenos Aires), the Saint-Marin (Imola), English (Silverstone) and European Grand Prix (Nurburgring).

1983. Jean Alesi at 19, during the «Marlboro looking for a driver» operation. He will be classified second.

# Chapter 1

# *The Roots of Passion*

Sicily, in the autumn of 1951. Frank Alesi is barely 11 years old, when he announces to his father that he loves automobiles more than anything else, and that he aims to make a career for himself out of his passion. Frank's father is amusedly shocked by this declaration; after all, their family has always worked in the neighboring vineyards. In this tranquil rural setting, the family had always worked hard, finding value in a day's work and a job well done. What's more, the Alesi family didn't even own a car, so how was it that his son was so suddenly smitten by cars, these rare novelties that seldom pass through the village.

Frank's father had always wanted only happiness for his children, so when his son decided to leave school to begin an apprenticeship as a body worker at a local garage, he was not excessively enraged. He has three kids, and told himself that he'll push the other two to finish their schooling. The Alesi family had always been a clan of passionate folks, headstrong in their desires, and it was best that Frank was allowed to dedicate himself to his love for automobiles.

In 1958, at age 18, Frank Alesi tells his father of his intention to leave Sicily and to being a life in France, for by this time, it had become quite difficult to start up one's own affair and try to turn a profit, as the Mafia stalked precisely those whose businesses prospered.

Frank's father was one to put his faith in fate. His philosophy was to leave to the fortune of his three children to chance, "If that's what you want to do, go to France, my boy." With that, he paid Frank's ticket and got the necessary authorizations for Frank to strike out on his own (Frank was still three years younger than the 21 years of age that constituted majority status).

When he was 19, Frank finally arrived on French territory with two of his mechanic buddies, one of whom had a cousin who lived and kept a bar in Carpentras, 30 kilometers from Avignon. So the trio headed off to join the cousin in Carpentras, where they soon found work in a garage.

Nevertheless, the group of friends quickly disbanded. One went back home to Sicily; another sought out even farther horizons, leaving for America; while Frank Alesi stayed, got married and opened his own garage in 1963, at just 23 years of age.

Frank, a motoring enthusiast inside and out, had gotten behind the

9

wheel of a roadster only shortly before 1961, when he signed himself up for a few regional weekend rallies. During the week he worked hard at the garage, an it was amidst this passion for the motor car that the Alesi children, Jose, Jean and sister Marie-Catherine but called Cathy, spent their formative years.

The senior Alesi being frequently overloaded with work at the garage, the children's education became his wife's task. It was she who escorted the kids to school and took care of all the details of child-rearing. She also kept the books for the garage and was often about the garage with her brood. During school breaks, the Alesi children spent a good deal of time in dad's body shop; and over the years, they virtually stewed in the scents and sounds of the auto shop.

From a young age, Jean revealed a turbulent side of his character. Contrary to his brother Jose, who was quite calm and attentive to the demands of others, Jean had trouble controlling his wild streak. "Mom always had more trouble with Jean than my sister or me," Jose remembers, "Jean didn't like school too much. When he had a good teacher, he proved to be one of the best of the class, but if he didn't like his teacher, it was bound to be a long, hard year. In any case, Jean always preferred recess to class time...

Jean's attitude had certain traits that aggravated his mother, who recognized that he was quite gifted, but unmotivated to work or to explore his intellectual capacities. For example, he refused to learn to adequately speak or write English at school, which became a delicate subject that lead to incessant arguments within the family circle.

Jean finally left school at 16, to complete a vocational training certificate in a year's time.

The Alesi family spent weekends in the racetrack's sidelines, supporting Frank. The three children were exposed to the racetrack-virus from the youngest age. "True, Jean has always been familiar with passion for driving. I liked it as well, but I was less talented behind the wheel," Jose confides.

When Jean had finished his schooling, one of his father's associates, a certain Mr. Gache, the father of Phillipe Gache, another adolescent destined to be a race car driver, told Alesi senior that he was going to let his son race go-carts. If Frank wanted to, Jean could share the cart with Phillipe, which would keep costs down for both parties concerned.

Frank accepted his offer. From 1981, Jean worked in the garage during the week, and raced go-carts each weekend, in what was called the "blue class" at the time, in the "Provence Alpes Cote d'Azur" league.

In his first year, 1981, he was the vice-champion of his league; his second season would earn him the league title. Today, Jean admits that go-carting never was his cup of tea. He raced go-carts only because he didn't yet have his driving permit, and go-carting was the sole means he had to get behind the wheel.

The year he won his first champion title, Jean was finally 18 years old and could drive real cars. In accessing his go-cart results, Frank Alesi realized that Jean had talent, and offered to help him compete in the Renault 5 Alpine Turbo Cup in 1983. Jean was excited by the prospect, and content to leave go-carting conclusively behind him. This was Jean's first year of circuit races, the R5 Cup being based upon 12 matches held throughout France. Jean wasn't familiar with any of the tracks, which wasn't an advantage when faced with adversaries of which a number were Formula 1 veterans. He won just one race, at Nogaro, held in a pelting rain that disadvantaged the track's regulars. Jean finished the championship in "the first place held by a driver not racing Dunlop tires."

For the 1984 season, Frank Alesi thought it better that Jean focus upon single-seaters. After all, it is with them that every driver's future lies.

Jean took part in the Elf circuit series, while open to the prospect of an entire season in Formula Renault. However, he finished second behind Eric Bernard, after a controversy arose that the race officials still remember: coming to the end of the circuit, Jean Alesi and Eric Bernard had to each finish a series of five laps subjected to a regulation time trial. Regularity being one of the Elf series' objectives, the victory was based upon the addition of these times.

Jean completes his laps without taking any risks, followed by an Eric Bernard driving just a bit faster, who takes risks and spins out, eliminating him from the race. The crowd moves toward Jean to offer congratulations, when the judges of the circuit decide that the last lap should be re-raced by the two competitors. This time, Eric Bernard finishes 1 hundredth of a second faster than Jean, and he is awarded the victory. Jean takes the decision as a profound injustice, and certain members of the judge's jury, twelve years later, admit to having made a terrible mistake at that moment.

For Jean, this loss means he will have to finance his Formula Renault season. This means he'll have to find outside sponsors, because one year of competition in single-seater was beyond the means of Frank Alesi.

Jeans finished the first three races of the season with what he considered a mediocre pit crew. The crew's boss was a con man who provided him with a non-functional car for exorbitant sums. Frank Alesi told himself that, for those prices, he might as well do everything himself.

Frank bought a new Martini chassis, and hired a retired grease monkey to develop the mechanics of the car.

In 1984, in his first season, Jean finished in second place one time in his "home-made machine." In 1985, he shoots for a spot amongst the big shots of the Formula Renault, Eric Bernard and Erik Comas. In the end, Jean finished fourth in the Championship, rather disheartened by the cheating that predominated throughout the season – Renault and Elf monopolized and controlled the championship, and had the marked tendency to favor their drivers, as far as material was concerned. Often, Jean was the fastest in the Friday time trials, before he was left in the dust the Saturday and Sunday. His car was always slower on the straight-aways, which left the Alesi family believing that perhaps the material was not exactly the same for all the competitors, contrary to the basis of the Formula standard model.

Frank had always followed his son on all the race circuits. By the end of 1985, he'd had enough of all the shady characters who frequented the Formula Renault. He met with the men from the Dallara pit crew, who had achieved real success in the Italian Formula 3 championship with their cars. Frank offered to Dallara to race their cars in the French Championship, thereby importing their chassis, to which were tied Alfa Romeo motors. All assembly and tuning of the total machine would be completed in the Alesi garage.

By this time, Jose had finished his schooling, and was working in the family autoworks. He took care of the administration of the pit crew, the ordering of parts and the importation of material. Jose was also the one in charge of finding the sponsorship necessary to finance the entire operation. These sponsors were regrouped under the title

"Competition Industry," that the S.N.P.E had organized at first, and at the heart of which were found brands such as Technirama, Bouverat and Mediaco.

At this time, the Formula 3 French Championship was supported by groups such as Martini, Lola or Reynard. For the Alesi clan to cross the start in a Dallara posed a certain challenge.

For the first race of the 1986 Championship, Jean finds that his starting position third from the grill – the first pleasant surprise. At the green light, he succeeds in taking a lead from the first turn. And stays in the lead for an entire two thirds of the race, to every one's surprise. But Jean's unseasoned nerves can't take the pressure, and he cracks, letting Yannick Dalmas pass him, and finishes second over-all. At the podium, Dalmas was quite surprised to have won a race he was sure was going to Jean.

Jean had to wait for his third championship race before making his mark at last. In the end, Jean would win two races this year, and he'll finish runner up to the champion, Yannick Dalmas.

In 1987, after noting Alesi's talent, Hugues de Chaunac approached Jean. The Alesi family understood that Jean's future lay in a totally professional structure like that of De Chaunac. Moreover, De Chaunac was sponsored by Marlboro, which permitted Jean entry into the closed circle of the cigarette manufacturer, one of the leaders in autosports material.

The Oreca pit crew was based in Magny-Cours, and raced Tico Martini's cars. In any case, from the first practice session at Albi, it was evident that the automobile was crippled by defaults. Jean can't doing anything with it; and Jose, who had kept its original structure, was suprised to see it finish fifth.

Hugues de Chaunac couldn't bring himself to believe that the Martini was the problem, even if one of Jean's teammates, Jaques Goudchaux, another Marlboro driver, was also baffled by the car. For the second race, at Nogaro, Jean asked to drive the car that Jose had assembled. Jose had an engagement with a driver, who had already paid for the first four races of the season. After De Chaunac himself asks to borrow the car for one race – in inventing a story that one had to know the car to know what its driver is worth, he had Jose re-negotiate with his driver. The driver gave his car to Jean for the Nogaro race, as Jose had offered to make him five cars for the same price if he would be willing to do this.

From the get-go, in his brother's car, he merits the pole-position. No one caught up with him throughout the race and he wins decisively. Faced with these results, Hugues de Chaunac accepts to buy two Dallara chassis. These chassis weren't readily available, and the men had to wait until after the next race to receive them. Jean was in agony over this, and finished fifth over all. The Dallaras get to Oreca for the race in Dijon. From this point on, Jean wins one after another the remaining seven races. When he reaches the Grand Prix F3 in Monaco, which serves as an opening act for the Formula 1, and permits the best of the Formula 3 from several countries to come head-to-head, he finishes in second place behind Yannick Dalmas – the position he had held during the entire race. Jean was crowned the French Formula 3 Champion for 1987. At the end of the championship, Marlboro organized a selective trials race for all the European Formula 3 drivers. The race was held at the circuit at Donington, and went to the same Formula 3000 driver who had just taken the championship.

# Chapter 2 — *Formula 3000 Champion*

Jean finishes with the best time of the day, which persuades Marlboro to offer him a budget to race the Formula 3000 series. En 1988, he finds himself competing in the Formula 3000 alongside Pierre-Henri Raphanel and amidst Hugues de Chaunac's Oreca pit crew.

The pit crew's month of March was not a pleasant one. Johnny Herbert, in a Reynard chassis, won everything. After waiting out five races, Hugues de Chaunac finally succumb to the pressure administered by his drivers, and bought two Reynards.

They came just in time for the circuit at Pau, where Jean got right up onto the podium. In any case, the season as a whole wasn't something to write home about. The cars proved to be very difficult to tune, and the more the pit crew worked to develop them, the worse they performed. For Jean, the 1988 season was rather mediocre, marked by numerous defaults and accidents. He describes his season with one word, "Catastrophic."

For his part, Jose continued to operate his little Formula 3 organization. He had raced the season with Eric Chely, who would finish second over all, in a close finish between Eric Comas and Patrick Leazar. For the entire season, the crew had counted only one default in 25 starts...

Jose planned to participate in the F3 Grand Prix in Macao, with Eric Chely behind the wheel. At the last moment, Chely declined to race. Jose told Jean that he had one place for Macao, and all he needed was 20,000 francs to get there. "Finally, I told Jean, 'Come on, let's go – I'll make you an advance,'" remembers Jose. This proved to be an ingenious offer. In Macao, Jean will meet Eddie Jordan, who would go on to take the Formula 3000 title in 1989.

"Macao was a little special," recollects Jose, "Petrol was unlimited, contrary to the French Championship; and everybody had special engines, as well as diagonal tires by Yokohama, that Jean wasn't used to working with." In spite of this, the small French team comes out of the time trials quite honorably, Jean qualifying for the first two lines.

The race was based on a compilation of times from two matches. At the start, a general pile-up immediately stops the race. Jean came out of it with a smashed front fender. Upon the second start, he takes off superbly, going directly to second position after the first turn. He holds this position behind the lead driver, awaiting the second round. In the second match, Jean starts in third position at the first corner, then moves up into second place. Since the winner of the first match had already dropped out, Jean was assured a victory at the finish line. Until he blew a tire on the last lap, and that forced him to finish at reduced speed, sick at heart.

Eddie Jordan had attended the race, and at the end of the circuit, he found Jean and Jose to ask them what their plans were for 1989. "Theoretically, we thought we'd stick with Marlboro, even if Jean's 1988 season had not been spectacular. And this is what we told Eddie. Since he was 100% Camel, this prevented Jean from driving for him. But then Marlboro Europe decided to cut off our funding, so we went with Jordan in signing a contract for 1989..."

From his side, Eddie Jordan had already heard much talk about Jean. His performance in Macao only further persuaded him to hire the Frenchman. "I knew of Jean from his Formula 3 days, in 1986," Eddie Jordan recalled, "At the time, I had a Formula 3 pit crew in France that was lead by an Irish friend. We were friendly with Jose, and had given each other a hand from time to time. My friend told me to take a look at Jean, which is why I went to Macao. I'd seen him several times in 1988, during his F3000 season with de Chaunac, but it was hard to form an opinion of him on this basis. What's more, Jean spoke very little English, so it wasn't so easy for us to communicate. In any case, I can say that we got on well. In 1988, I finished third in the championship with my driver, Martin Donnelly. We were pretty optimistic about 1989, and I must say that we made up a highly respectable pit crew.

However, it's not until after Macao that Eddie Jordan was firmly decided to sign Jean on, "Yes, I wanted Jean, but he was known for being pretty difficult, to be honest. People said it was hard to make him do what you wanted. I, myself, think that this reputation was well-earned, but that aspect of his personality didn't bother me in the least. That type of guy doesn't worry me. Often, it's even better to work with someone with a strong character. From what I'd heard in the pits of the F3000, Jean was someone who followed his emotions: sometimes really quickly, and sometimes to his detriment. Furthermore, I'd heard he wasn't very good at tuning his cars. I can tell you that I was pleasantly surprised to see him at work. He was infinitely better than rumor suggested at fine tuning, he was even very quick and his work consistent.

Jean still had his pool of sponsors support for 1989, amongst others were Bouverat, and the companies Max Mayer and SNMI.

When he'd taken Jean on, Eddie Jordan also signed a management contract with Jean. "He was very friendly with the people at IMG (International Management Group, McCormack's team in London)," Eddie Jordan goes on, "And he needed some help in getting his career on track. Jose took care of his business, and I took it upon myself to introduce him to all sorts of people, like Frank Williams, Ken Tyrrell, etc.

For Jose, who had served as Jean's "manager" up until then, saw the agreement with Eddie Jordan as insurance for the future, "Since Eddie was the director of the pit crew that Jean would work with in 1989, and the other driver, Martin Donnelly, was also Irish, Jean and I decided it would be better to sign a management contract," Jose explained, "This would only prevent Eddie from favoring Martin over Jean, even if it was done unconsciously. Eddie is an excellent businessman, and I can only say nice things about him. We've always been on good terms and consider him a friend.

In spite of this, 1989 did not start under the best auspices. "We'd had many doubt-filled moments from the start of the year," Jose admits. "The car wasn't very dependable, and there had been problems with the universal joints, then the brakes, etc. Luckily, Jean got along really well with Paul Cosby, his engineer. They formed an excellent team."

Eddie Jordan also remembers perfectly the difficult debut, "Jean had two or three horrible races, where he made some errors. At the Silverstone, he finished fourth, and he defaulted at Vallelunga, when he could have done better both times. Some of my men were literally furious with him. Personally, I'd prefer to forget it. I had him come to England, to the factory. I showed him all the guys who worked so hard to make him his machines for each weekend. I told him it did me no good that he was a hero in the streets of Avignon; that he needed to work out, get himself into shape. I don't think he really appreciated my speech, but he knew I had Camel behind me, and Marlboro had just dropped him. He had to make an effort, or watch everything go up in smoke...So he came to my place in Oxford to live for a while and learn English until I found him an apartment at the end of the street. I think his stay wasn't as terrible as he thought it would be at first. Furthermore, he won the next race, at Pau. He realized then that his efforts would pay off...

At Oxford, Jean proved himself a diligent student in English, a language he had reasonably assimilated two months later, after spending entire days working at it.

His Formula 3000 season started looking up. At Jerez, he finished fifth, before he finished second at Brands Hatch and won one after the next the races at Birmingham and Spa. Upon his arrival at Mans, he needed only one point to take the title of Intercontinental Champion in Formula 3000. He earns this last point in finishing sixth in the race. He won one race at the end of the season, the same day as the Portuguese Grand Prix in Formula 1 was disputed.

He didn't compete in the final race of the season at Dijon, for by then he had already made the change over to Formula 1 with the Tyrrell pit crew. He had already participated in a few Grand Prix since the month of July in their company, but that's another story (refer to chapter 3).

The year of 1989 proved to be a busy one for Jean. In concurrence to his participation in the Formula 300 with the Eddie Jordan crew, and in Formula 1 with Tyrrell, Jean also races in the IMSA summer events, behind the wheel of a Ferrari F40 with the "Meichelotto" team. Rather by hazard had Jean Sage, an official of Ferrari France, put together this affiliation. The race track at Laguna Seca, just south of San Francisco, where the event was held, allowed Jean to discover the West Coast of the US. Jean found the sum of these factors to his liking, and he finished third.

A little earlier in the year, Eddie Jordan had reserved Jean a spot in the Japanese Formula 3000 Championship. He went with his engineer, but managed to blow the engine during the run, and considers the entire ordeal a negative experience. "To tell the truth, he found everything about Japan to his disliking," Jose recalls. Since then, it would seem Jean has changed his opinion on the subject

# Photo legends

| | | | |
|---|---|---|---|
| Page 17 | Jean Alesi in his Formula 3, in 1987. He brought home the French Championship this year in a car assembled and maintained by his brother, Jose. | | Palmer; and just in front of his old rival from the Volant Elf, Eric Bernard's Larousse. |
| Page 18 top | Jean at the 24 Hours on the Ice in Chamonix. The man from Avignon has taken part in this annual race since 1984, before he became an ice-driving instructor. Sometimes, even a wall made of ice can cause damage. | bottom | To everyones surprise, Alesi's Tyrrell-Ford finishes in fourth place. This sensational debut will earn him the nomiker, "rookie of the year." |
| | | Page 25 | 1990. The definitive revelation of Jean's talent, in his blue and white Tyrrell-Ford. |
| middle | 1987, during the F3 Grand Prix in Monaco, where Jean finishes second. | Page 26 | The American Grand Prix in Phoenix, the first match in the 1990 World Championships, the start. Jean, in the second line, takes the lead from the first corner, in front of Ayrton Senna. At the half-way point in the race, he enters into a tense duel with the Brazilian. Alesi's legend stems from this race. |
| bottom | 1985 in the Formula Renault. A difficult year for Jean; in a car managed by his family, Jean took a place on the grill alongside big teams financed by Renault and Elf. | | |
| Page 19 | At the 24 Hours on Ice in Chamonix. | Page 27 | The podium at the same event, and second place behind Senna. |
| Page 20 top | 1988 and the Formula 3000 with Hugues de Chaunac's Oreca team. A laborious season... | Page 28 top | The Grand Prix in Monaco 1990. Again, second place after Ayrton Senna. |
| bottom | The Alesi's Garage in Avignon, where Jean's roots lie. | bottom | At the steps of the podium, the happiness in newfound glory at one of the most prestigious Grand Prix. |
| Page 21 | Jean's family (nearly) altogether. Mom, Dad and Jose, the oldest brother, confident and manager of Jean's affairs. Missing is younger sister Marie-Catherine. | Page 29 | Grand Prix in Monaco 1990. Panorama shot of the Loews corner. |
| Page 22 | In the streets of Pau. This win put Jean on track to win the title of Intercontinental Champion of F3000. | Pages 30-31 | The 1990 season is no more peaceful for Jean, who passes a difficult summer, stuck between Tyrrell, Ferrari and Williams. |
| Page 24 top | Friday, July 7, 1989. At the age of 25, Jean competes in his first Formula 1 with Tyrrell. In the time trials, he takes the 8th line, 6 tenths behind his teammate Jonathan | | |

# carrosserie alesi

**MATMUT**

**GROUPAMA**

VEDENE 90 31 02 14     AVIGNON 90 86 32 59

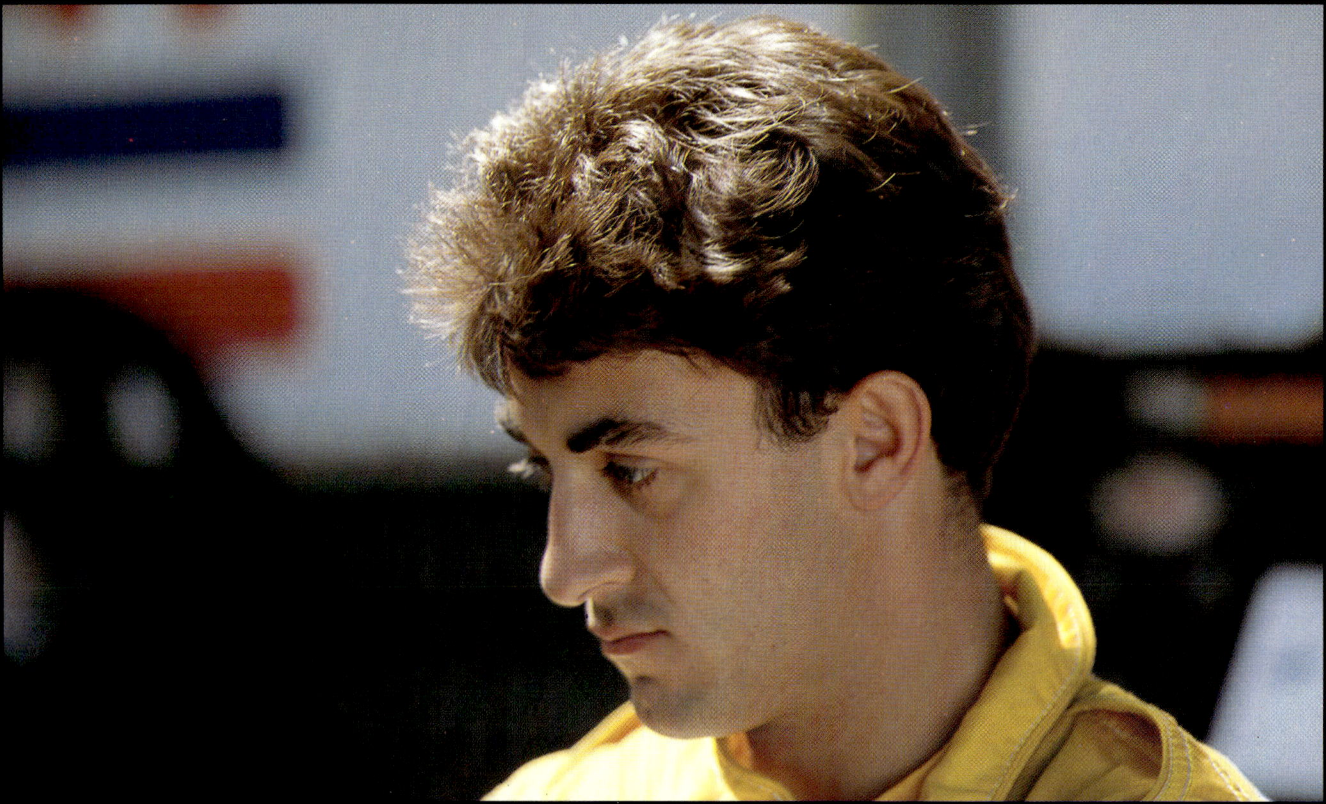

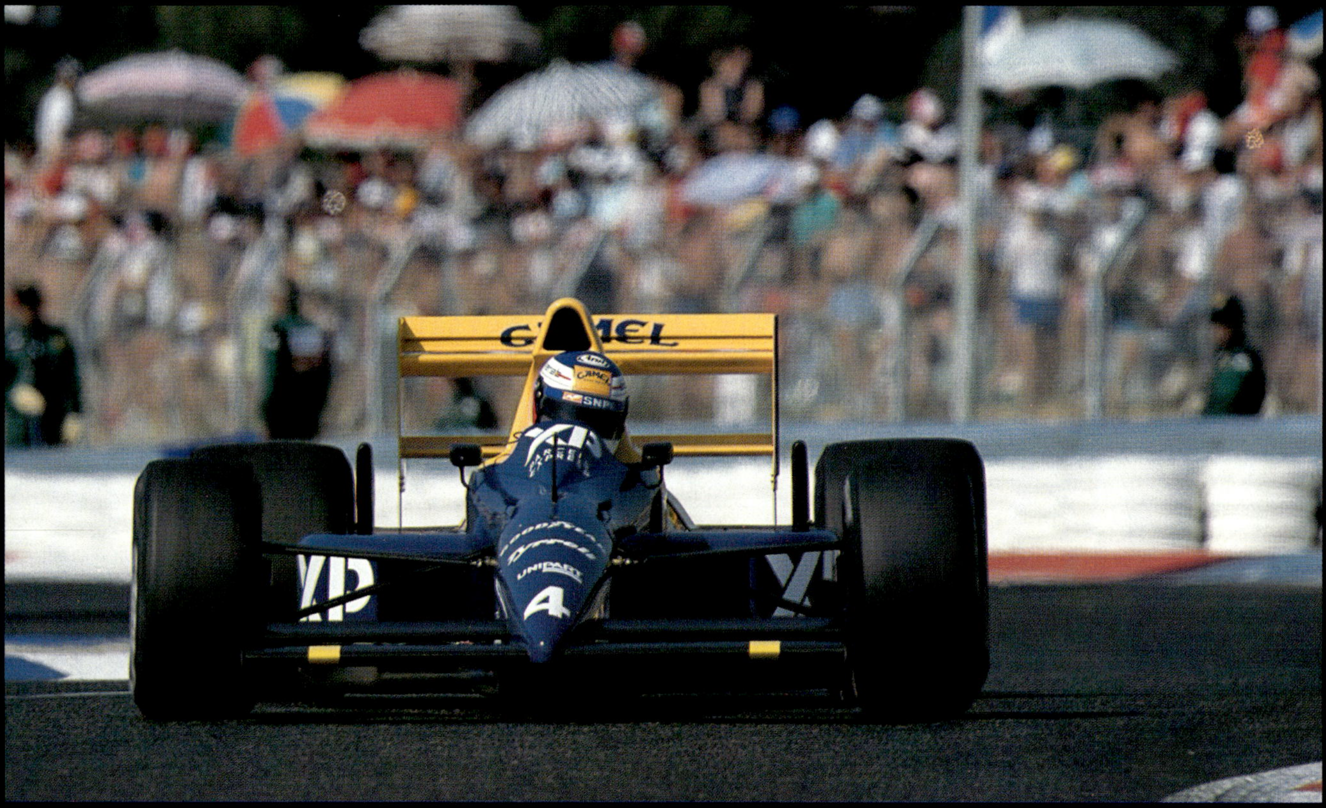
UNIPART
4

ICEBERG
FORMULA
CHAMPIONS
ICEBERG U.S.A.
PRIX
NIX ARIZONA
EPSON
Marlboro
HONDA
NACIONAL
RENAULT
Canon
elf
DENIM

MAGNETI MARELLI
ellesse
Agip
PIAA
ALESI
EPSON
PIRELLI
4

PIRELLI
EPSON
Marlboro

# Chapter 3 — *Formula One with Uncle Ken*

In 1989, Ken Tyrrell coordinated Michele Alboreto and Jonathan Palmer to drive his two single-seaters. The team had two excellent engineers at its disposal in the Frenchman Jean-Claude Migeot and the Englishman Harvey Postlethwaite – both of who would later execute their skills at Ferrari. Unfortunately, the enterprise lacked sponsorship. The Tyrrell 017s were first painted black, then a solid dark blue, which made for a beautiful product, a product whose financial future was as somber as the car. In spite of the money set-backs, Michele Alboreto succeeded in scoring a few points, notably by finishing third in the Mexican Grand Prix. This allowed Ken Tyrrell to land a huge contract with Camel, who thereupon became the crew's principal sponsor, adding its name in large gold letters to the hood and fenders of the blue mobile. "I was very happy to have reached that agreement," Ken Tyrrell remembers, "But Michele (Alboreto) wasn't. He had always been with Marlboro, and wanted to remain loyal to them. He left in the middle of the season, and I had to find someone else.

Ken Tyrrell carries the reputation as a skillful talent scout. Once again, he makes the call in hiring Jean Alesi. But he admits it was really by chance. He never heard of Jean before the end of June 1989, "...It's true, I didn't even know the name. When I started looking for a pilot, I naturally turned to the Formula 3000. I asked around to find out who were among the best drivers. When someone told me 'Jean Alesi,' I said, 'Who in the heck is that?' I called Eddie Jordan after learning that he was Alesi's manager, Eddie told me that he thought Jean would be interested in racing a Grand Prix F1 or two.

Eddie Jordan perfectly recalls the call he got from Tyrrell, "At that time, I was managing Johnny Herbert and Jean Alesi, amongst others. Herbert was already driving for Benetton, and I wanted to place Alesi with Arrows. Derek Warwick, who was driving for Arrows, had just hurt a leg in a car accident, and I called Jackie Oliver to offer Jean to him. That's when Ken called. Since he was with Camel, like myself, the deal was easier to arrange with him. We needed the okay of Duncan Lee, the competition director at Camel, but he was in Siberia for the Camel Trophy, and I had a heck of a time trying to get a hold of him. When I finally got him, I told him we needed to put Jean in a Tyrrell. He was okay with that. I was as happy as I'd been when I succeeded in placing Martin Donnelly, my other driver, in an Arrows...

At the time, Jean competed in the Formula 3000 championship with Eddie Jordans team. His driving style had already made waves in the discipline. "Jean had a very peculiar style. He seemed to be all over the place, in a state of permanent state of loss of control, but that was just his style. I'll admit now that when I hired him, I'd never thought that he'd be up to bringing home a championship. And he's done it. We'd become good friends. We share lots of similar interests in life, and we've spent a few of our vacations together, in Spain and Germany. I think it helps a lot if the director and the driver of a team are good friends.

Thanks to Jordan's efforts, Jean ends up in the stalls at the French Grand Prix at Castellet, completing his first Formula 1 in the driver's seat, a particular Thursday the 6 of July 1989.

"We hadn't even done the tests with him yet," Ken Tyrrell relives, "We simply didn't have the time. The first time he drove the car was at the Friday practice sessions. I'd told him that I'd be very pleased if he qualified the car. But he did much better than that: he qualified for the eighth line, and finished in fourth place. I was really happy to be so lucky, because before the course, I'd had him sign a contract with options in my favor for the three following seasons. I still do this with my young drivers.

In 1989, Jean ended up disputing eight Grand Prix for "Uncle Ken." In fact, he finished all of them except for one, that conflicted with his Formula 3000 schedule. "Ken Tyrrell had him sign a race-by-race contract," Jose says, "he paid Jean 50,000 francs a Grand Prix.

At the end of the 1989 championship, after having competed in only half of the races, he was already in ninth place overall, with eight points. A more-than-brilliant debut. Considering these results, Ken Tyrrell exercised his contract option that guaranteed him Jean's services for the 1990 season. For the young man from Avignon, who had just taken his first Formula 3000 title, his first full season in Formula 1 looked quite promising. He had to race the first two Grand Prix of the season in the 018 chassis from last season; The new 019, with its new and unique design that added broad wings to the front of the chassis, wouldn't be making its track appearance until the Grand Prix at Saint-Marin.

Moreover, the Tyrrell crew arrived in Phoenix for the season starter with an added worry, since the team had switched from Goodyear tires to Pirelli at the last minute.

In any case, the circuit was on city streets, which forgave the few defaults in the chassis. This enlarged margin for error allowed Jean to qualify in the practice sessions for the second position, next to Andrea DeCesaris, but behind Gerhard Bergers Maclaren and Pierluigi Marinis Minardi.

At the green light, he shot off like a rocket, and slipped his Tyrrell into the lead at the first corner. He kept the lead for 34 laps. After Ayrton Senna caught up to him, he relinquished the lead only after a grueling duel in which the two men passed and re-passed one other several times. The Alesi "legend" was born.

Jean finished second, at mounted the podium for the first time in his Formula 1 career. After the final, he received more media attention than Senna himself. Journalists and television teams all wanted a word from the new hero. Yet Alesi was very calm after dismounting the podium to tell his tale, "Everything worked well, the car was perfect," he says, in a manner that leaves one thinking this is old hat for him, "I started on intermediate rubber that held well. It started to slip a little when Ayrton caught up to me. Normally, I would have let him pass me, because he was obviously faster than me. But when he passed me, I saw a chance to get back in there, and I told myself, 'Why give up without a fight?' And I went for it. I'll admit it was a little risky.

Ayrton Senna had no beef with his young rival, and had enjoyed the fight, "There wasn't much room between us, it's true, but the fight was fantastic, and cleanly fought. I love what I do for a living after races like that. That's what automotive sport is all about.

In any case, Jean was not intimidated in the least by the prospect to have battled with the great Senna, who was already the one-time world champion, "I'll admit that it was a dream of mine to find myself racing against Ayrton, to see him in my rear-view mirrors," he'd said the evening before the race. "When I raced the Formula 3, two or three years ago, he was already achieving amazing feats in the F1 with Lotus, and he was my hero. He still impresses me today, but I have to try to beat him; it's my job.

In Brazil, for the second Grand Prix of the season, he qualifies in seventh place before he finishes seventh place overall, due to a stroke of bad luck after an attack by Nelson Piquet, "Obviously, it wasn't easy," Jeans remembers, "my tires were completely finished, and my engine is less powerful than Piquet. I couldn't keep up, and I had to let him go...

At Imola, with it's "motor circuit" reputation, Jean was able to again qualify the Tyrrell-Ford for the seventh grill position. Here, the 019 made its first appearance on the track designed by Emilie Romagne. The design adhered to the new technical regulations of the season that came into play from the start of the Italian race. The winged-nose design from aerodynamics specialist Jean-Claude Migeot stood clearly apart from all the other F1 vehicles, whose designers wasted no time copying the design innovation.

Jean described the new mounting as, "Comfortable and easy to drive." And he proves this by taking the point that comes along with sixth place.

Next is the Grand Prix in Monaco. With a 100% urban track, like that in Phoenix, Jean Alesis fans begin to gather 'round, expexting another exploit from their idol. He does nothing to calm their excitement by declaring the week prior to Monaco that he thought he was in the position to take the pole! "I like when people talk about me," he said at the time, "that doesn't throw me off balance, it motivates me!"

Already in the time trials, he's looking fierce, and wins third place on the starting grill. He had held onto second position behind Senna for a long time before Alain Prost sneaks his Ferrari right in front of him. "Starting from the second line is always a handicap here, for sure," he comments audaciously, "but the car was great, and I'm staying very optimistic about the race. If I can take the lead at the start, nobody will see me for 45 minutes, thanks to our Ford motor that lets us carry 50 liters less that the competitors with V10 or V12 engines.

At the race start, the green light goes, but Jean is not able to take the lead at the first corner. Ayrton Senna and Alain Prost are sly devils who won't let him get past them so easily. Still, Jean will commit the exploit of the day during the race a little farther along in the first lap.

"Jean really impressed me with his performance in Phoenix," Ken Tyrrell remembers, "In my eyes, he enacted two fantastic feats in 1990. At Phoenix, of course, he'd been able to take the lead behind the wheel of a feeble car with a 20-year-old engine, and this in a race against the best driver, in a McLaren with a V10 Honda motor...But in my opinion, Monaco was where Jean pulled off his greatest stunt. After the start, he was able to pass Prost in the breaking section before the hairpin turn at Mirabeau, to take second position behind Senna. Berger sees him succeed in this advance, and tries to do the same thing, setting off a general pile-up. Okay, the second start is given, and our Jean does the exact same thing to Prost, in the exact same spot. He had to do it. It was incredible. Fine, he finished second, and third in the drivers' championship, but it was a wonderful day.

The rest of the season was unfortunately not as joy-filled for Jean. In Canada, He went off track after bumping Andrea DeCesaris. At the Mexican Grand Prix, he finished seventh, before he goes down hard at the French Grand Prix. It was Jean's first anniversary of his arrival on the F1 circuit, and he can't reproduce his results from 1989, "I knew it would be harder than my first year, he explained, "But not this hard." Because of the Pirelli tires that were totally useless on the new surface of Paul Ricard's circuit, the Avignoner had to be content with a seventh line position on the grill. After two laborious days of trials, "I'd really had to push it to the limit. What else can I say? There's absolutely no traction to speak of." He was forced to default the race after blowing the differential.

The rest of the summer was not any more positive for Jean. In England, he'll finish eighth, outside the winner's circle. In Germany, on Hockenheim's track designed for powerful motors, he is able to catch up a little and qualifies his Tyrrell in eighth place.

In the race, he still achieves nothing, and finishes eleventh and last place, more than five laps behind the winners.

In Hungary, the sinuous track gave the Tyrrell driver a touch of hope; He clocks in with a time that affords him a place in the third line of the trials, and that could end up being the pole position. On Friday, he holds onto the top of the ratings, until he's displaced by Berger and Mansell, "The car was fantastic," he bubbles, "the tires are perfectly balanced, and finally, the qualification tires finally lasted an entire lap." On Saturday, he would lose a little ground to finish sixth on the grill.

In the final, he unfortunately locks up with Pierluigi Martini, where he loses a lap.

In Belgium, he returns to faster tracks where his single-seater is less efficient, and he finishes eighth.

Next is Monza. Jean Alesi is of French nationality, but everyone from the peninsula is well aware of his Sicilian roots. The Tifosi are more enthusiastic about his performances than anybody realized they could be during his negotiations with Ferrari for 1991.

After the fans had waited so patiently, Jean wasn't to let them down. In the practice session, he races an incredible fifth time, to the ovation from the crowds amazed to see him finish a second faster than Senna on a circuit not wonderfully suited to the Tyrrell-Ford's strengths. "Yes, I'm quite surprised by my car," he explained, "it works perfectly with the Pirelli qualification tires, which, for once, lets me concentrate on driving the car instead of fine tuning it." In the final, he goes no farther than the fifth lap. Starting off well, just behind the two McLarens, he was all over the track trying to keep the pace with them, holding on to Gerhard Bergers tail, with every intention of passing him at the first opportunity, but he gets carried away and exits the track in the fifth lap.

At Estoril, Jean finished eighth. Then he left the track again at the Spanish Grand Prix after Gerhard Berger clearly pushed him into the gravel, "The worst part was that Ron Dennis came to see me at the starting grill to tell me to stay away from Berger, who was behind me. At first, I kept my line, but he was all over me. I tried to put some space between us, but he touched my wheel and the rim broke. Dennis should stick to giving his advice to his own drivers.

At the Japanese Grand Prix, Jean had to forfeit after leaving the track violently due to a ruptured steering cable. Contrarily, he was in good shape for Adelaide, the last Grand Prix of the 1990 season. Third at the end of the first day of practice runs, he qualified in the end for fifth place after serious brake problems – the circuit was extremely demanding on the breaking system, and at the time, Tyrrell was the only team not using disks made by the French brand Carbone Industrie.

In the final, Jean can't do better than eighth, and finishes the championship season in ninth place – all thirteen of his points being scored in the first four Grand Prix of the year.

Alesi then left Tyrrell for Ferrari. For "Uncle Ken," it was a huge loss to see his star driver go like this, "Jean was an amazing guy. Basically, he loves to drive," Ken Tyrrell says today, "He's and inspired driver; and in fact, he still has trouble believing that he gets paid for doing it. He thinks it is outrageous that he gets paid to drive a Ferrari in a Formula 1. Everyday is Christmas for him, and I like him a lot for his appreciativeness. We were really good friends when he drove for us; and we still are...

"I also liked his driving style very much – it's really spectacular. He loved the qualies. That was when we still had qualification tires, that lasted only one lap. Jean really liked that, because he liked to give everything, to go all out for one lap, to hedge all your bets on such a limited space in time. On the other hand, he didn't like the private qualifications of that time. He thought it was really boring, and frankly hated the Grand Prix distance tests. But I liked him a lot, even if I couldn't keep him...

During the summer, Jean was taken up in a maelstrom that will carry him as far as Ferrari, in 1991. This was a decision that held heavy consequences for him career. The races in red would now begin...

# Chapter 4

# *The Move to Ferrari*

In 1989, Jean was called "the rookie of the year." The results from the 1990 season proved that he was more than just a flash-in-the-pan. He'd shown he was made of the stuff of champions. Ultra-quick, precise, consistent, whole-hearted and efficient. He had so many qualities, that they didn't go unnoticed amongst the crew directors. His performances in Phoenix had caught every one's attention, and in the end, driven Jean to the point of dismay when faced with the task of choosing a pit crew for the 1991 season. He made a name for himself amongst the public in just a few weeks, and many already claimed he was the qualified successor to Alain Prost.

During the summer 1990, the rumors running rampant regarding his future began to affect him to the point that even his driving performance was perturbed. During the month of July, it seemed the Alesi had more to occupy him off the track than on. The crews in the stalls of the Formula 1 couldn't stop the interrogation concerning the choices he would soon be forced to make: the guessing had placed him with Tyrrell, Williams, McLaren, Bennetton and even Ferrari for the 1991 season. Anguished, he was forced to give an impromptu press conference one Friday to clarify the situation, "I'm going through a difficult period right now," he explained before a group of journalists who wanted to hear him state who he would drive for in 1991, "I'm having trouble concentrating on my driving, and that's why I've gathered you together to tell you that I haven't decided anything concerning my future. I'd like that you let me finish this season in peace with Tyrrell before we start discussing next year. I'm the one driving, I'm the one taking the risks, and nobody will make me make a decision. I've always managed my affairs with Jose, and I intend to continue in the same fashion.

Ken Tyrrell, who was at his side, took advantage of the moment to reaffirm his intention to keep his prodigy for the following year. "As I've said before, I have a three-year contract, with options in my favor. Yet, at the end of 1990, Jean asked me to not exercise my option. I don't know anything more than what I've read in the press. Obviously, Jean didn't tell me about his contact with Ferrari or anyone else. And I didn't need to talk to him about it, because as far as I'm concerned, I already had a contract with him.

Ken Tyrrell frowns in recalling these old memories. The episode is still painful for him, "When I knew Jean was leaving, obviously, I wasn't really happy. Because once more, I gave a kid a chance, and he dropped me like brick when it suited him. No, I never took him to court...I've never done it and I never would. Experience has taught me that it is useless to try to keep a driver who wants to go. If he doesn't want to drive for you, it does no good to try to force him. He won't give his best, anyway. We could have made a little money suing Ferrari, but we didn't. It would have been too long and difficult to justify doing it.

Eddie Jordan, who was still Jean's official manager, remembers well the circumstances that lead to Jean signing on with to drive for Ferrari, "Everything began right after the race in Phoenix, where Jean battled with Ayrton Senna. I'd spoken of him with Frank Williams several times since I'd started taking care of him, even before he began the Formula 1. Frank called me and asked to meet Jean. We talked a long time, then I asked Jean to come to England to meet Frank. Really quickly, and very early into the season, Jean signed a three-year contract with Williams. It was a solid contract for Jean, who hadn't yet disputed 10 Grand Prix. It was a fantastic opportunity – nearly too good to be true.

Everything would have held if Jean hadn't been approached by Cesare Fiorio, the sports director of the Scuderia at the time. "For Jean, Ferrari had always been a childhood dream. I couldn't do anything to tear him away from the idea. The Friday night of the trials at the English Grand Prix, Jean and Cesare Fiorio met for a long time. I was absolutely furious. Jean knew I didn't want him with Ferrari. I thought it too early in his career. But Jean talked all the time about going to Ferrari, and so off he went. He signed a second contact with the Scuderia. What's more, I'm not 100% sure that Cesare Fiorio knew about the contract with Williams.

Ken Tyrrell entirely agrees with Eddie Jordan on the fact that Jean made a mistake signing on with Ferrai, "He made a huge error. I don't say this in light of the success Williams has had since, but because he wasn't ready to drive for Ferrari. During his first two years with them, he didn't improve. He was too inexperienced. They paid him well, no doubt better than Williams would have, but he shouldn't have given in to the siren's song, even if it was hard to resist.

Once the contract with Ferrari was finalized, Frank Williams became genuinely outraged. He announced publicly to journalists that he had a contract with Jean and that he expected to see it honored, "I signed a contact with Jean the 2 of February 1990," he thundered, "I understand that he prefers driving for Ferrari, but first and foremost he should have kept his word. We can't always have what we want in this life. I'd like very much to walk again tomorrow morning, but I know it's impossible."

Master Henri Peter, the Scuderia's Swiss lawyer, was able to keep the noise down and avoid creating a scandal: a financial agreement seemed to been arrived at between Ferrari and Williams.

Amongst the Alesi family, the affair didn't happen in exactly the same way, "Sure, we signed a contract with Frank Williams," Jose admits today, "but the contact carried performance clauses that would have been hard for Jean to live with. At any time in the season, Frank Williams had the right to replace Jean if he so desired. We knew that at the Hungarian Grand Prix that he'd signed with Riccardo Patrese, and that he'd proposed a contract to Ayrton Senna, who went directly to show it to Ron Dennis, who was obliged to raise his salary. Furthermore, Frank Williams was discussing with Nigel Mansell. Jean told me he didn't think Frank would hold him to it; then, Ferrari offered us a solid, three-year contract, covering from 1991-1993. With them, Jean would be working with Alain Prost, who was then leading the race for the world title. When we signed with Ferrari, in September, the two Williams drivers, Patrese and Mansell had already signed, which meant that Frank Willliams no longer needed Jean. That's why Williams never pursued the case. If Jean had stayed with them, he would have been relegated to a lowly test driver.

Hindsight being 20/20, it's easy to see that soon after, Williams enjoyed infinitely more competitive success than Ferrari, but Jean has no regrets. "With things like that, you must never have regrets," concludes Jose, "Ferrari provided Jean with invaluable experience, as well as an international image that he would have never had with Williams. To drive for Ferrari carries a prestige all it's own. In my opinion, that's exactly why Michael Schumacher decided to go to Ferrari...

During just his first year on the Formula 1 circuit, Jean had already experienced some of his career highs and lows. After the joys of finding himself mounting the podium in Phoenix and Monaco, the Frenchman had to face the worst situation a driver can know, lost between contracts with Tyrrell, Williams and Ferrari.

At the end of this debacle, Jean understood what the term, "the price of glory" meant. He had been simply too brilliant behind the wheel, had too many people vying for a piece of him, and had to pay a large price.

Fortunately, the ending to this affair was the happiest from Jean's point of view. In 1991, he would drive a Ferrari. It was a child's dream that he would have never dared imagine could become reality at the moment his dad Frank Alesi brought him to his first go cart races.

# Chapter 5

# *First Red Missiles*

The 1991 season began in Phoenix, Arizona, the American showplace for the Grand Prix. All winter long, the Ferraris had dominated the inter-season practice sessions, and they began the 1991 season the big favorites. On the basis of the results from 1990, when, by the end of the season, Alain Prost had made very clear that his vehicles were superior, no one knew who would be capable of beating the Scuderia's single-seaters. They had two of the best engineers in Jean-Claude Migeot and Steve Nichols, a colossal budget, and two drivers who complimented each other well in Alain Prost and Jean Alesi. The Scuderia had brought together all the elements for success.

For Jean, the year was heading in the right direction. His God-given talent in the hands of and with the support of Alain Prost would help him secure a place amongst the champions...

What's more, nobody from the competition seemed prepared for the approaching season. The winter's private trials had left many unanswered questions. One of these questions concerned the new McLaren MP 4/6 with its Honda V12 engine. It had come out very recently – so recently that the British pit crew had barely had the time to road test it. The car arrived in Phoenix more or less straight from the factory. McLaren was only to have gotten a hold of its materials at the very last minute. The new Williams FW 14 also had a limited number of miles on its tires. Its transmission was of a yet untested size.

On the contrary, Ferrari had spent a quiet winter fine-tuning its material for the following season. The 641 chassis had performed so well at the end of 1990, that Cesare Fiorio, the Scuderia's director at the time, had decided not to design a new car. He only wanted to improve the existing model by reworking a few details.

This would be a decision he would come to bitterly regret. From the first moment the teams made their materials known to the public, Friday the 8 of March, doubts began to infiltrate the red team. From the first free practice session of the season, Ayrton Senna in his McLaren, finished more than a second ahead of Alain Prost's Ferrari. "I'm quite surprised by the McLaren's performance," said an astonished Prost, "it's a car they put on the track for the first time only last week, and it's already highly competitive. It seems too good to be true...

On the other hand, nothing came easy for Ferrari. The tone was set for the season: it would again go to Ayrton Senna, who would bring home his third world title.

The party that the Scuderia had organized would soon be rained out; the 1991 season will remain forever engraved in the minds of the tifosi as one of the worst years in the history of the Scuderia, or at least it's grandest deception.

Heads would roll at the end of a season without results. After Commendatore Enzo Ferrari died in 1988, management of the Scuderia fell back to the FIAT group, whose technocrats didn't know much about automotive sports. For them, this lack of results would be paid for dearly by those found responsible.

It was Cesare Fiorio who had made the decision to keep the old chassis; thus, it was he who was to take the blame for Ferrari's failure. He was replaced by the start of the Canadian Grand Prix. He held Alain Prost responsible for his dismissal, after Prost had openly condemned him in declarations to the press. The management of Ferrari came under the triumvirate of directors composed of Piero Lardi-Ferrari, the Commendatore's son, Marco Piccinini and Claudio Lombardi.

However, changing a team's manager doesn't render a car any faster on the track. The serious inadequacies evident from the season's start, as well as the winter trials held without a direct comparison with the competition's materials, had effectively restrained the Ferrari team's performance. The situation wouldn't begin to rectify itself until the French Grand Prix, when the hastily designed 643 chassis would make its debut.

The chassis was far from perfect: it behaved differently at a start of a race than at the end, but it was still progress. Not enough of a progression, however, to allow the Scuderia to take back its position amongst the top teams who waited for no one. Ferrari had make huge changes from the very start of the season. The biggest improvements concerned engine function and fuels. Fueling was unregulated, and it seemed that Elf relished creating special fuels. The Scuderia tried to make up for the chronic lack of power its drivers had attempted to contend with. They required its fueling sponsor, Agip, to create an all-new line of fuels, that saw the day at the Hungarian Grand Prix. The gains in power were nearly non-existent, and the loss of engine reliability was astoundingly huge.

Illustrating this at the Hungarian Grand Prix, the motor blocs fabricated by Cavallino will crack, one after the other, decidedly putting an end to any hopes of the Scuderia making up for its previous losses.

As if this wasn't enough, the Italian press attacked with such savageness, that the team's cohesiveness was clearly affected.

It got so bad that at one point, Jean Alesi, who had previously kept silent in the face of Alain Prost's statements, will finally let it all out at the Portuguese Grand Prix, just before Alain Prost gets himself thrown off the team for publicly insulting his vehicle: he deemed it "an 18-wheeler."

Jean's first season with Ferrari was hard on him. He had hoped to race a loyal and sportsmanlike series, and instead had to cope with a year filled with controversy. Ferrari seemed more interested in personal problems than car racing. This profoundly disturbed Alesi and he recalls the year as a low-point for his morale.

For Jean individually, the year had gotten off to a good start. In Phoenix, at the season's first Grand Prix, he gave his all to please his new bosses. While Alain Prost was contemplating the McLaren's performances, Jean tried to follow to the advice Cesare Fiorio gave him to the letter. This worked relatively well, for the man from Avignon would find himself in temporary pole-position at the end of the practice sessions. Less than one minute after the checker flag unfurled, starting the series, that Jean will stop the clocks. "I must admit that I pushed it a little far," he states later, "but it was a dream lap. I was constantly at my limits, and I didn't run into any traffic.

By Saturday, the smiles were already long gone from the men from Ferrari's faces. In the morning, the two drivers agreed that their cars were not fit to drive because of the heavy fins that a street track like Phoenix requires. There was nothing one could do before the final, and it didn't help any when they realized that the qualification tires were destroyed before having finished even one lap.

In the final, after holding on to second position for a long stretch, Jean had to forfeit when he blew the transmission. It was Alain Prost who would finish in second place.

Two weeks later, in Brazil, Ayrton Senna was on home turf. He let it be known that he had every intention of taking "his" Grand Prix. In the practice sessions, he took the pole position, while the two Ferrari drivers were relegated to the third line, Alesi in front of Prost. Once more, on Friday, Alesi was capable of claiming the best time of the day, but he was defenseless on Saturday when faced with the McLarens and the Williams. In the final, he finished sixth over-all, and scores his first point in a Ferrari. "With a full tank, the car is okay. But once it gets lighter, it's really hard to drive. It's really lazy with its gear-changes, and I had to be rough on it to make a mark on the straight-aways. I stopped to change tires, but that only helped for the three laps that followed...

Jean thought that the decision to have stuck with the only slightly modified Ferrari 641 for the 1991 season was a blatant error, "It's obvious that our car belong to a past generation. It's really difficult to tune because it's far too touchy when it comes to regulating the suspension. The smallest millimeter of change radically alters the car's performance.

The excessive optimism that the Scuderia had known in Phoenix, had turned 180 degrees at Ferrari, to a pessimistic extreme.

Nothing changed at Imola. Five weeks had passed since the Brazilian event, and the polemic on the future employment of Cesare Fiorio as the head of the Scuderia was already a subject of debate.

At the starting grill, Jean slipped back another line, and now found himself behind even Stefano Modena's Tyrrell. In the final, both Ferrari drivers exit the track: Alain Prost during the warm-up lap, and Alesi in attempting a rather suicidal passage of Stephano Modena.

In Monaco, Jean finishes on the third step of the podium by sheer force. "It was hard work," he commented, "we'd made some rather daring last-minute adjustments. We risked everything with really soft shocks in front and lots of support. But that didn't work as we'd planned. It was unresponsive in the turns, and that wore on the tires. Under those kinds of conditions, I'm quite content to have finished on the podium.

At the Montreal Grand Prix, Jean arrived to find the Ferrari pit crew transformed, Cesare Fiorio's dismissal having immediate effects. After qualifying for the fourth line, he's forced to pull out of the race when he breaks the gear box.

45

The following race, in Mexico, was a disaster. The track was extremely bumpy: a real disadvantage for the Italian chassis. Jean is forced to stop in the 43rd lap after his clutch goes out.

Next is the French Grand Prix, which coincides with the arrival of the new Ferrari 643. After only four days of road testing, the Scuderia decides to put the car on the track at Magny-Cours. The drivers were overjoyed: the 643 should provide them with some semblance of a suspension system. Sunday, Alain Prost finished second, less than three seconds behind the winner, while Jean finished fourth.

At the Silverstone, the optimism surrounding the 643 dies down a bit. At the end of the final, in which both drivers were forced to forfeit after exiting the track, Prost states that this car responds exactly like its predecessor: perfect at the start of the race, becoming increasingly difficult to handle as its fuel reservoirs empty themselves.

At Hockenheim, Jean comes in third, complaining about the lack of capacity for top speed, being especially handicapping on the Hockenheim Autobahn.

The rest of the season didn't go much better. In Budapest, Jean scores two points by finishing in fifth place, at the end of a race he describes as exhausting. "My dashboard controls went out at the start of the race, then the engine started misfiring and lost power. I had to force it the entire race. I had to go all out for two little points. It's not much...

In Spa, Jean forfeits after his motor gives out; as he does again at Monza, two weeks later.

At Estoril, Jean comes in third again. This doesn't stop him from venting his fury against the Scuderias management, who seem eminently more interested in politics than auto sport, "We've got a lot of problems with the car at the moment, but the pit crew is more preoccupied with what Alain Prost will do next year than adjustments. What we need to be doing is working on the cars. What Alain will do is not my problem. I think he's gotten enough results in his career to do what he wants, but I wish he would decide, and fast, so we can get back to work. I'm the one paying for all of this hullabaloo.

Jean's angry outburst is over as quickly as it began, which is characteristic of him.

One week later, in Barcelona, Ferrari's performances had already markedly improved, and the cars seemed dependable again – enough that Prost finished second, and Jean came in fourth.

Alain Prost nearly left Ferrari for Suzuka, but the divorce from Ferrari would last only a few days. He would come back and race the Ferrari, still saying it was so bad that he might as well be driving a truck. The leaders at FIAT didn't think this was so funny, and sent Prost walking. The 1991 season finished in a state of total chaos. For Jean, it was time to turn the page, take a breath of fresh air...to buckle down and get to work on 1992 Ferrari model.

# Photo legends

| | | | |
|---|---|---|---|
| Page 49 | Jean's first run in the new Ferrari, on the Castellet track. Christmas comes on January 16 for Jean in 1991. | Page 59 | The 1991 season brought no substantial results. The rush was on to get the Scuderia's models to the winter trials in preparation for a better 1992 season. |
| Page 50 | First Grand Prix of the 1991 season, and the first problems. Here, the first day of times trials, deep in conversation with Alain Prost. | Page 60 | Impressions are exchanged with Jose after a testing session. |
| Page 51 | The splendor of Monaco's Grand Prix, 1991. | Page 61 | If 1991 was tough, 1992 was even tougher. German Grand Prix, Hockenheim, 1992. |
| Page 52 top | In the rain, Jean's always a bit ahead of the pack. Trials at the Saint-Marin Grand Prix at Imola, 1991. | Page 62 top | Jean being interviewed by his ex-teammate, Alain Prost, who now works for TF1 television. French Grand Prix, Magny-Cours, 1992. |
| bottom | In front of Alain Prost. Portuguese Grand Prix, Estoril, 1991. | bottom | One more race up in smoke. Spanish Grand Prix, Barcelona, 1992. |
| Page 53 | The 1991 season. After planting the seeds of hope, the year quickly turned to catastrophe. The mood was black at the Scuderia. | Page 63 | Going all out. Canadian Grand Prix, Montreal, 1992. |
| Page 54 | Jean often gets the crowd going; like at the Spanish Grand Prix 1991, where he pushes the limits... | Page 64 | In 1992, Jean didn't have the chance to make a lot of sparks. British Grand Prix, Silverstone, 1992. |
| Page 55 | Fighting nose and nose with Ayrton Senna. Spanish Grand Prix, Barcelona, 1991. | | |
| Page 56 top | A season of races at half-mast, 1991. | | |
| bottom | Alain Prost's irreplaceable support, the Hungarian Grand Prix in Budapest, 1991. | | |
| Page 57 | Jean doesn't find his place in the sun at the Italian Grand Prix: forfeit due to engine failure, Monza 1991. | | |
| Page 58 top | Mexican Grand Prix, Mexico City, 1991. | | |
| bottom | German Grand Prix, Hockenheim, 1991. | | |

GOODYEAR
Marlboro
Marlboro
Agip
MAGNETI MARELLI
WEBER
GOODYEAR
GOODYEAR

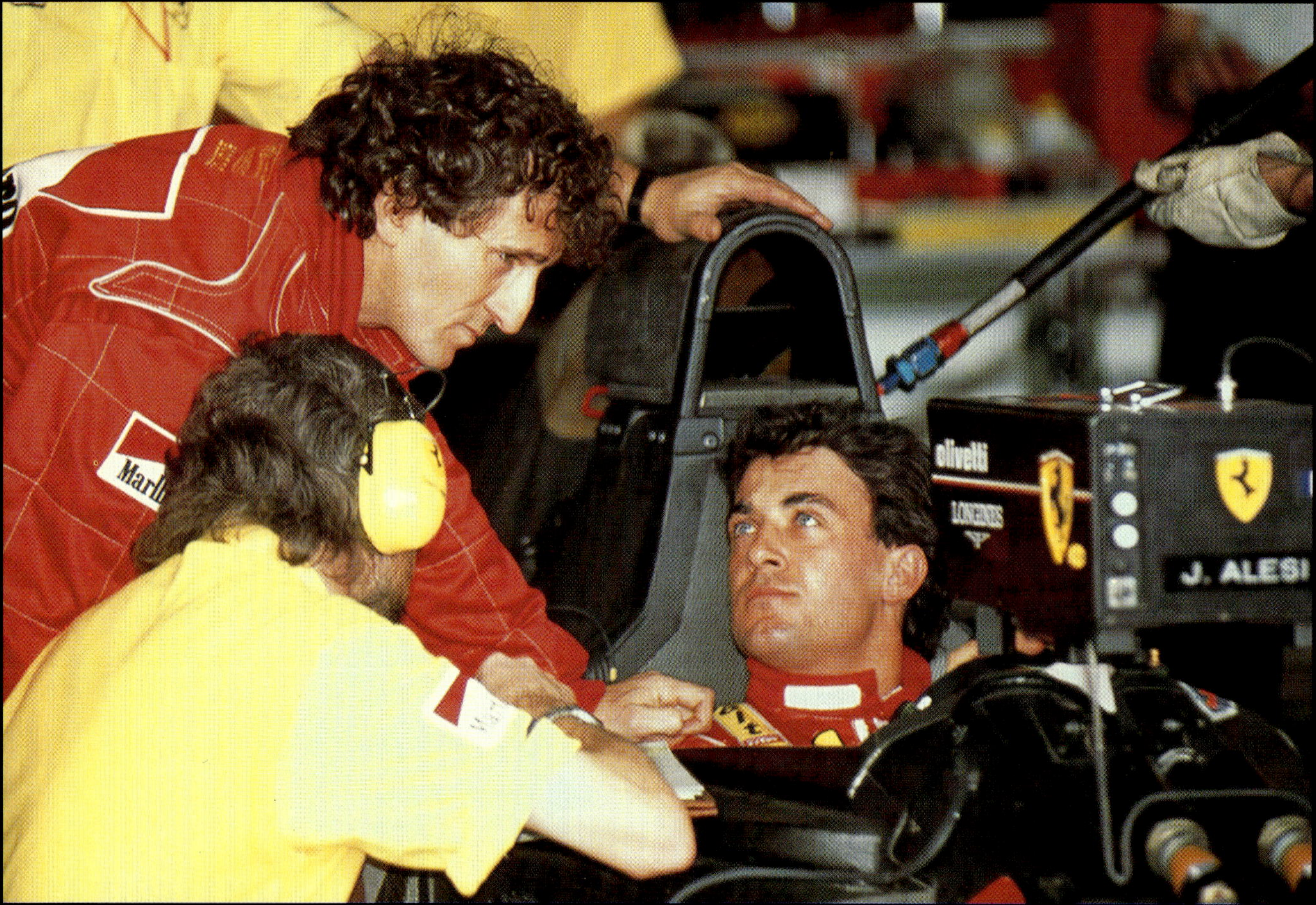
olivetti
LONGINES
J. ALESI

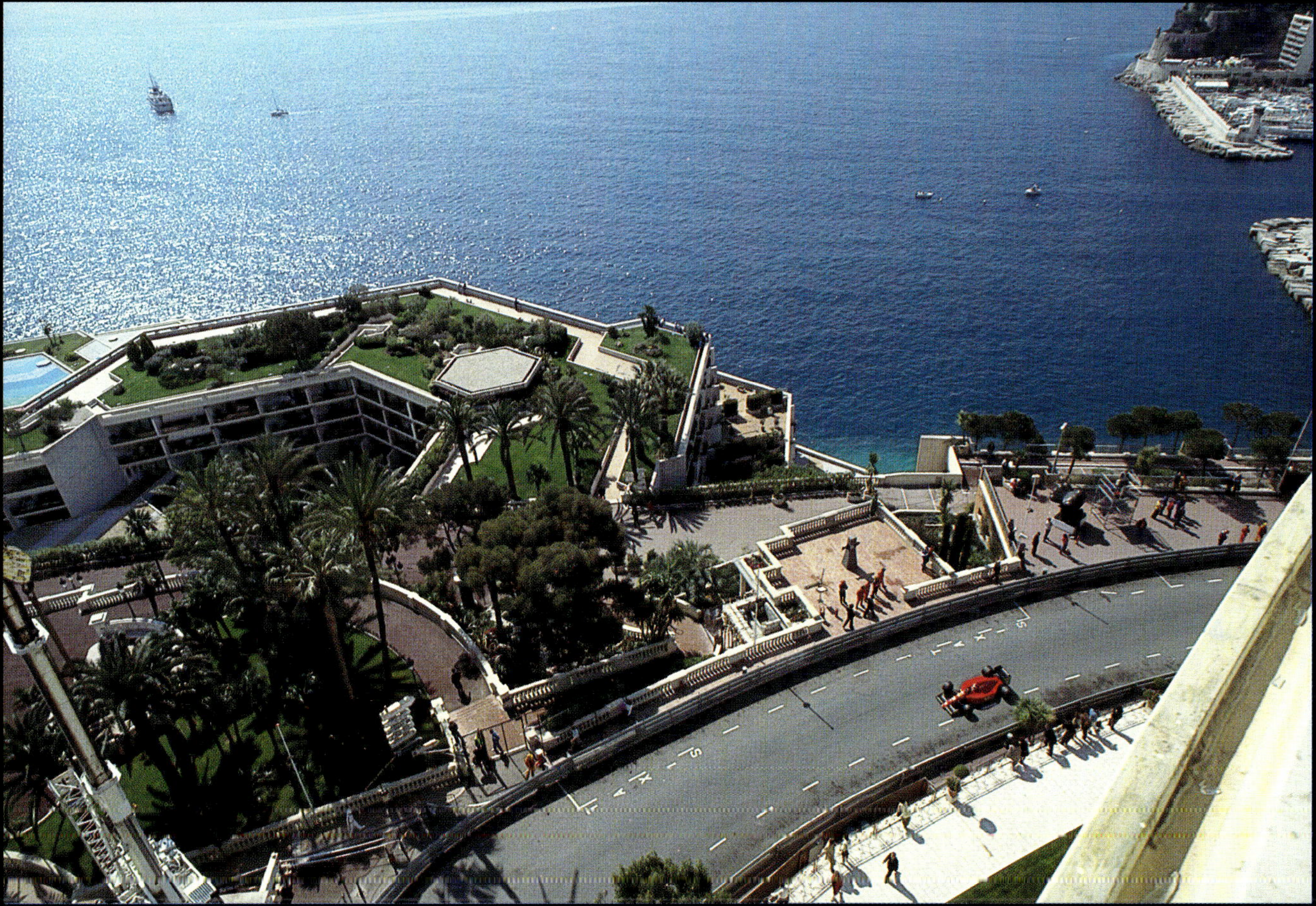

GOODYEAR
Marlboro
Agip
28
MAGNETI MARELLI
WEBER
GOODYEAR
GOODYEAR

Marlboro
8
GOODYEAR
28

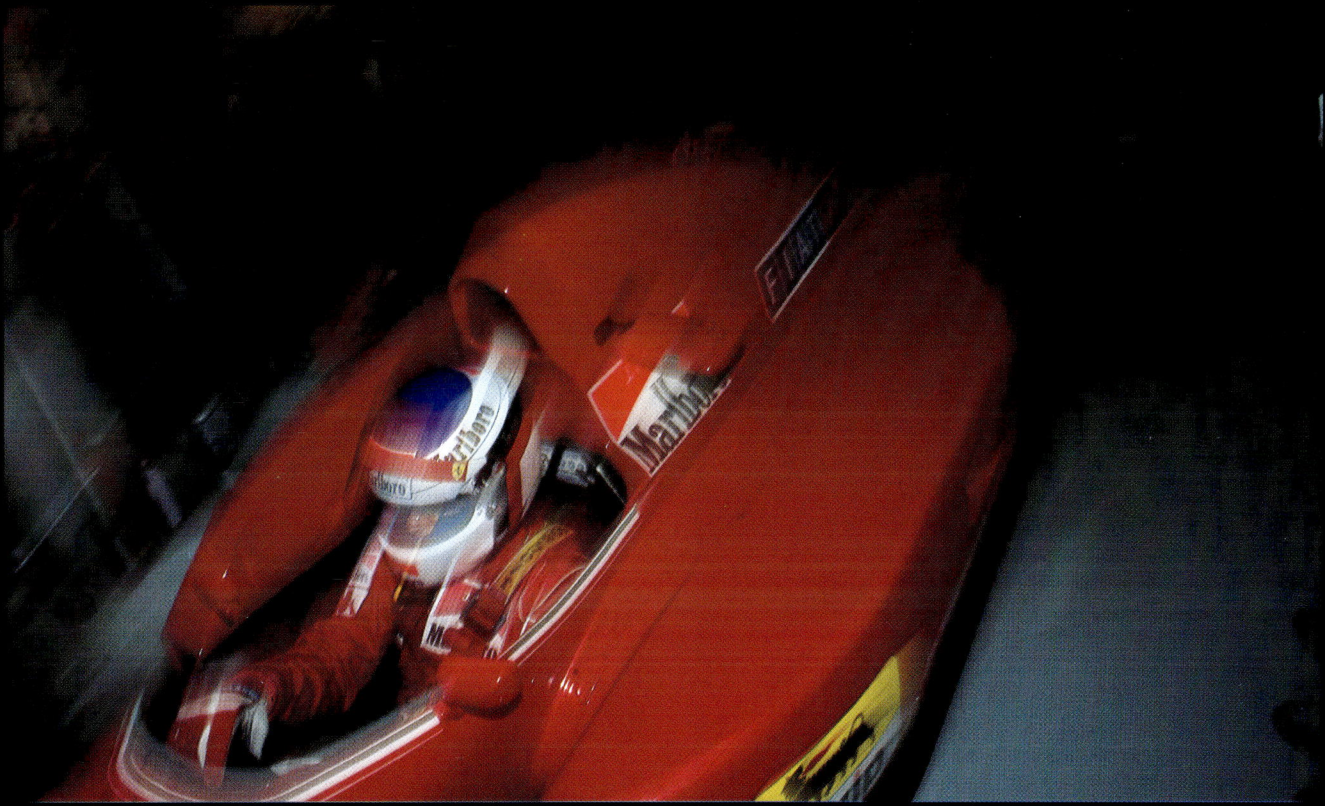

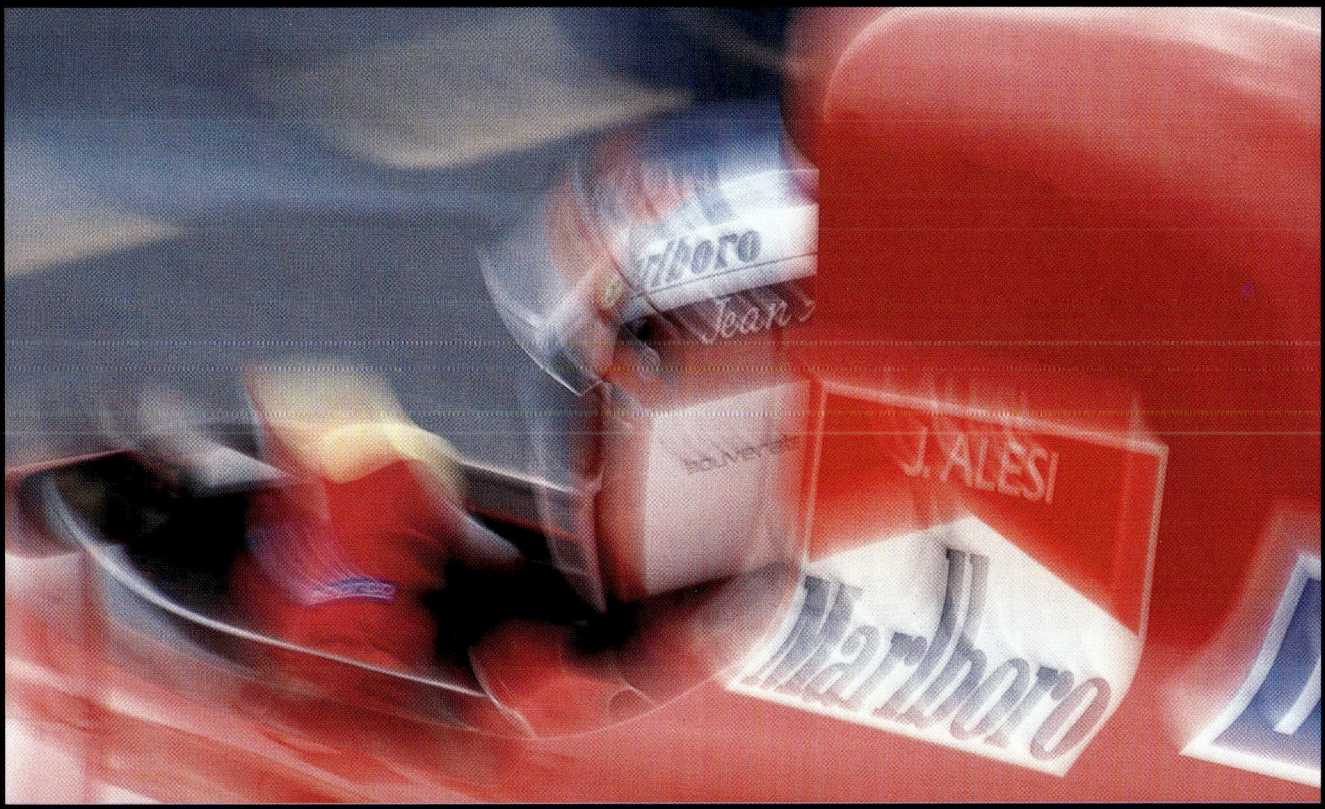
J. ALESI
Marlboro

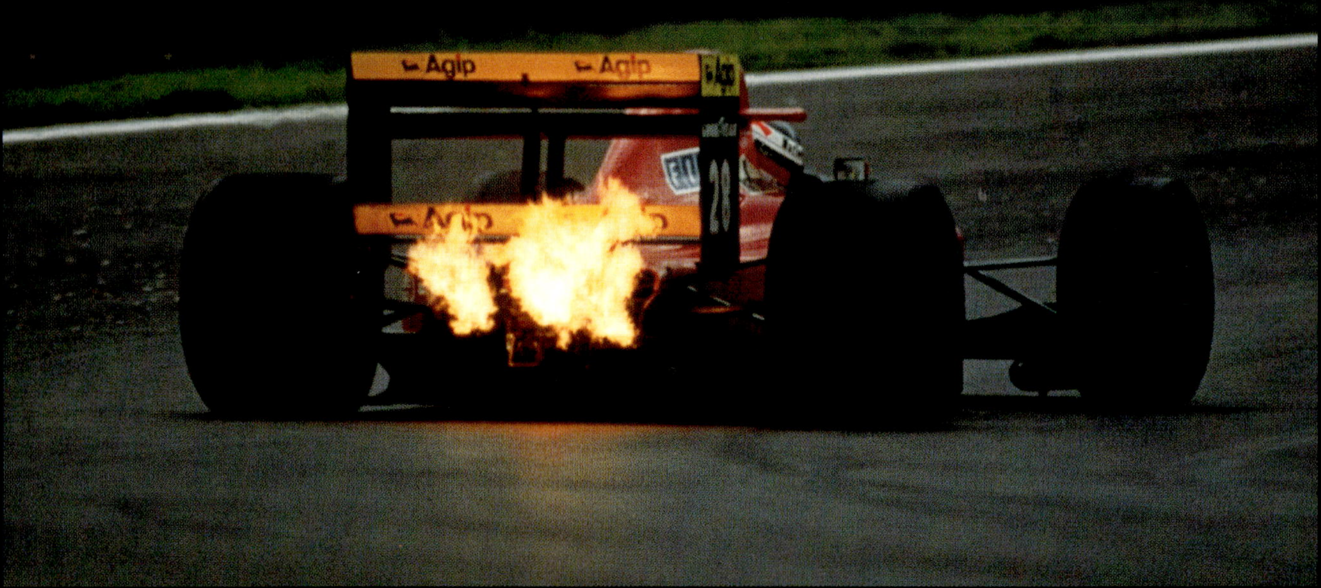
Agip
Agip
28

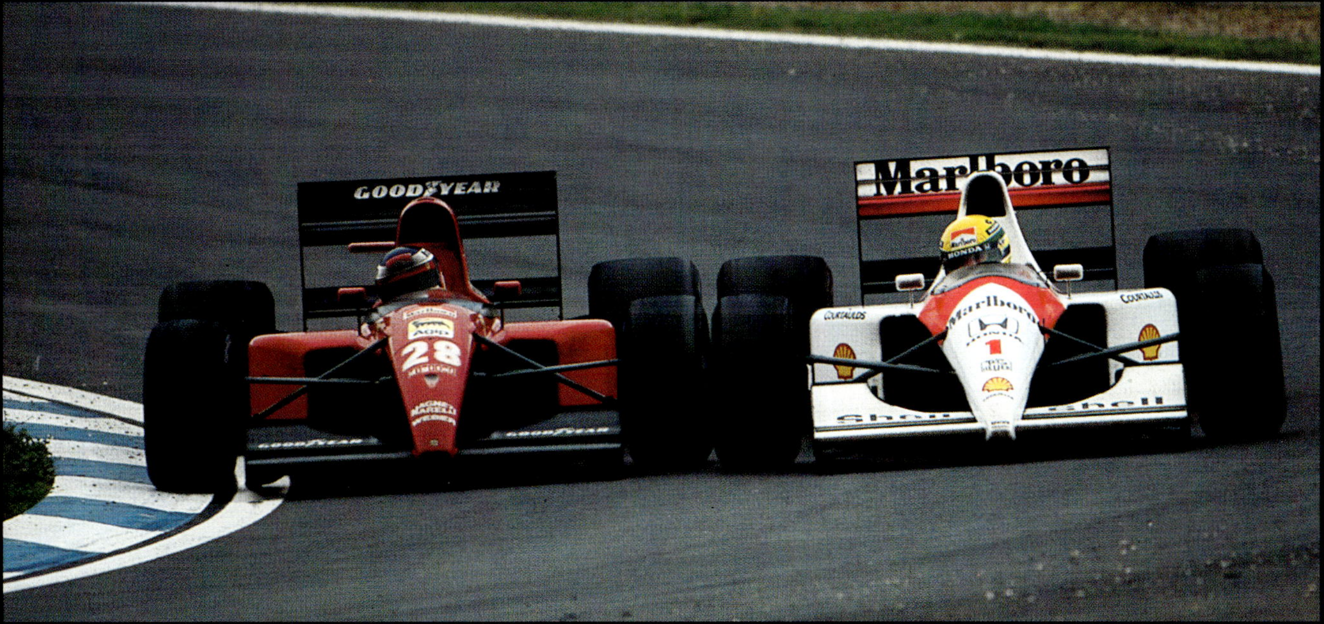

GOODYEAR
Marlboro
28
Marlboro
COURTAULDS
Shell

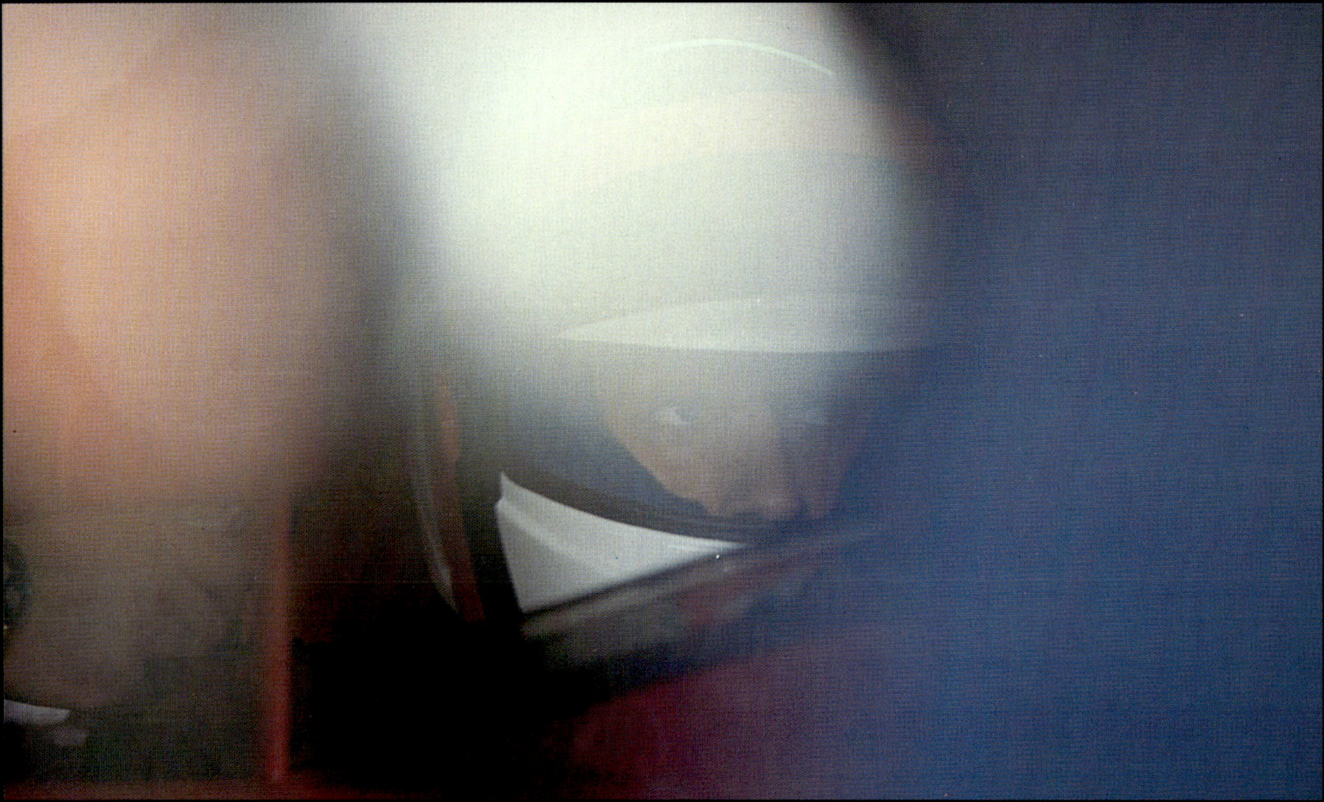

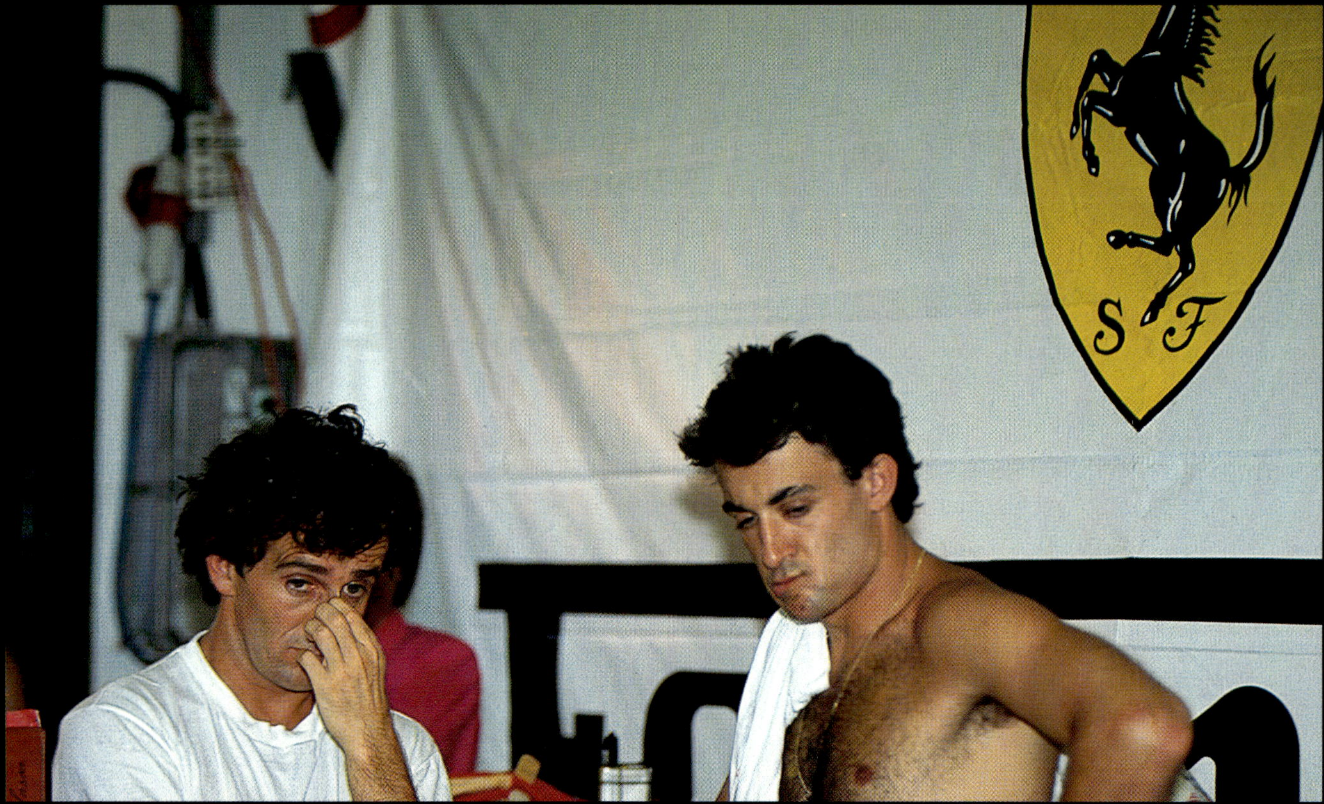
S F

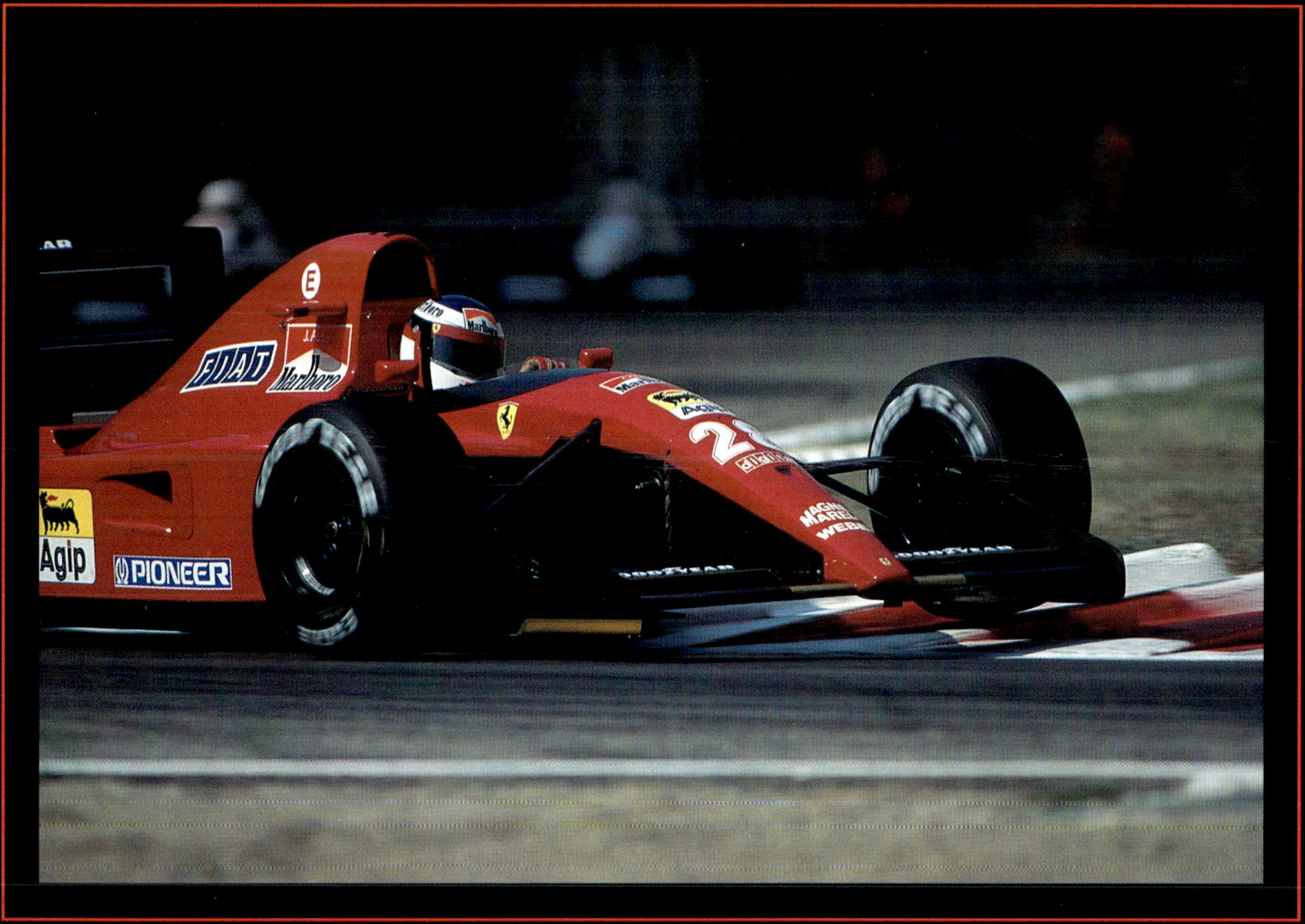
Marlboro
Agip
PIONEER
GOODYEAR

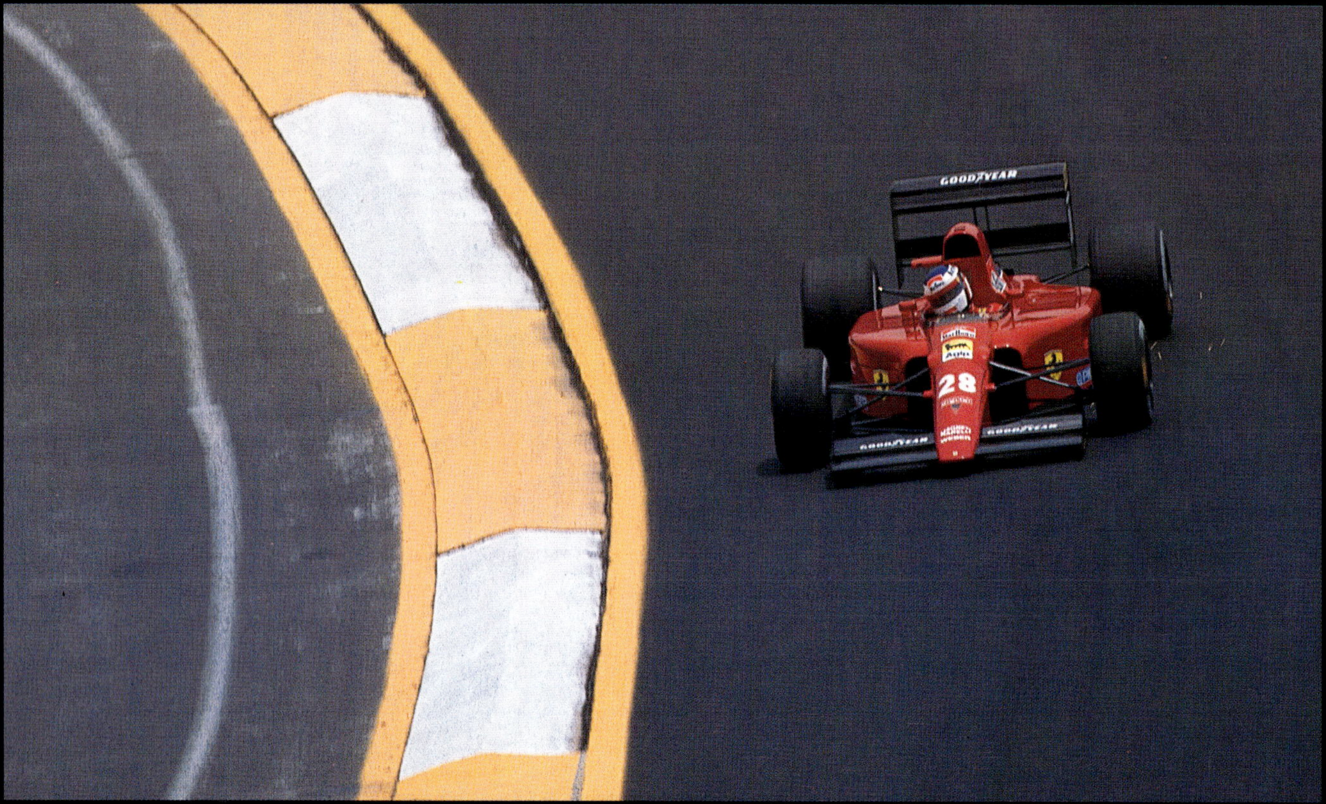
GOODYEAR
28

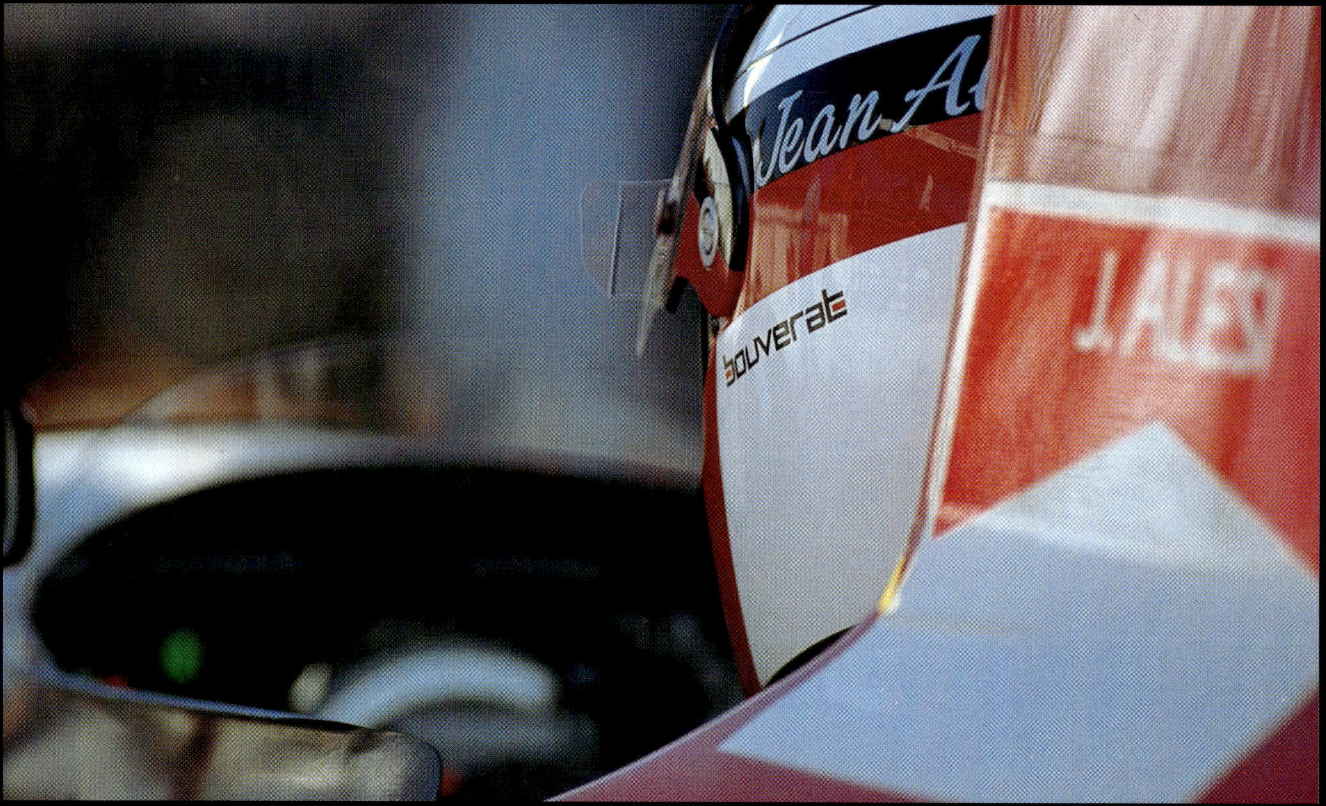
Jean A
bouverat
J. ALESI

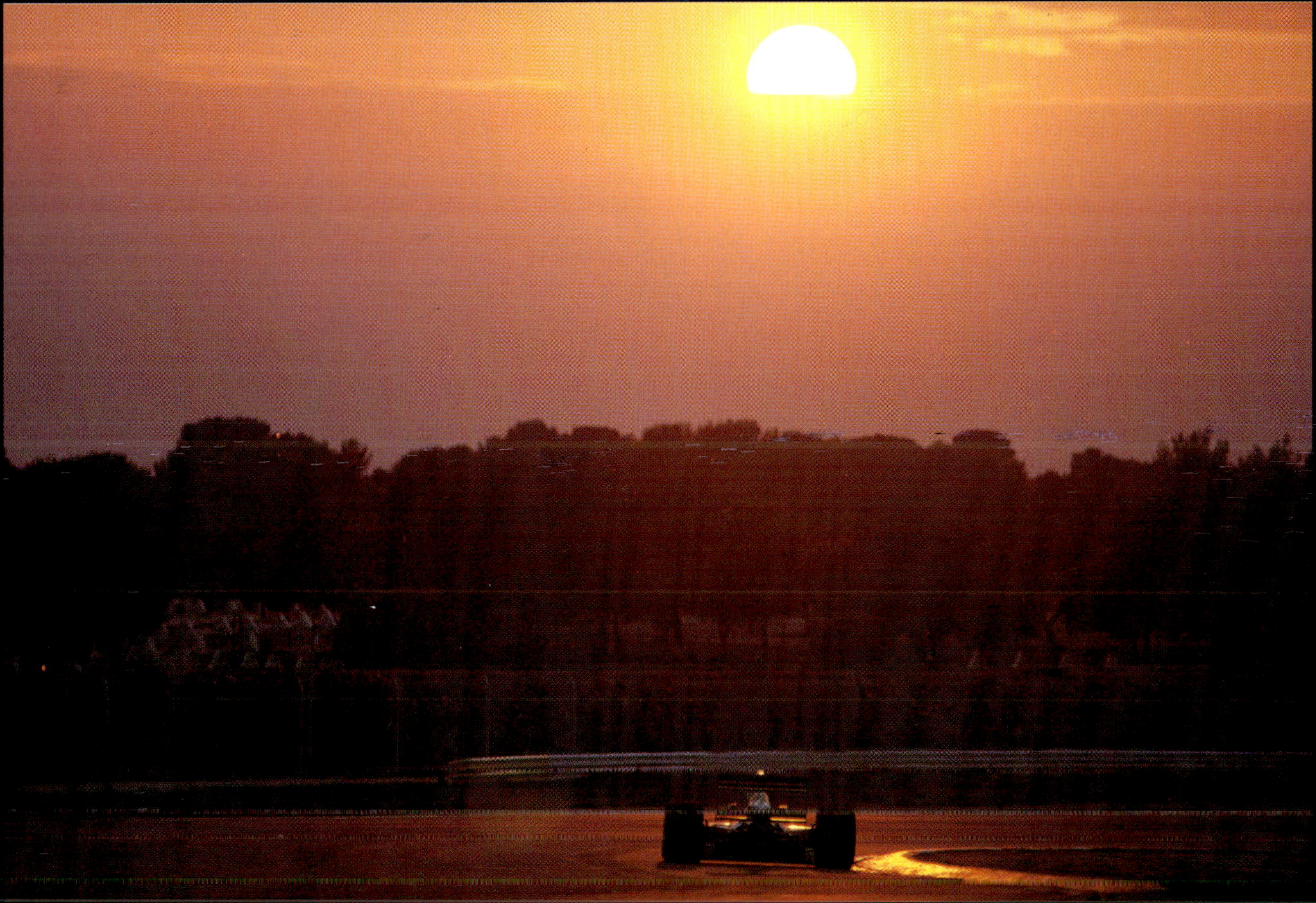

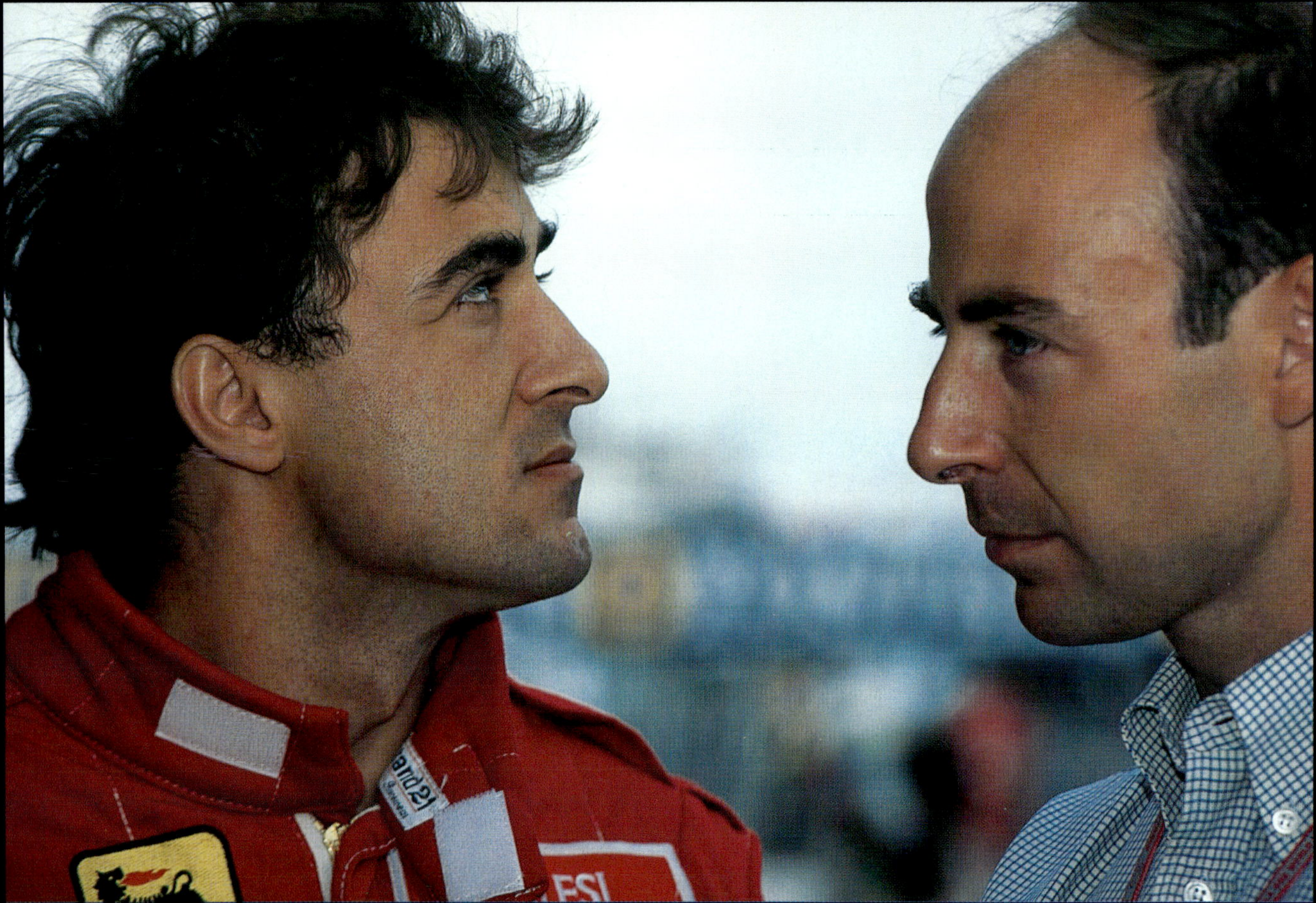

Agip
GOODYEAR
27
FIAT
J. ALESI
E
BBS
arexons
MAGNETI MARELLI
SKF
WEBER
PIONEER
Agip

TF1
NECMA
J. ALESI
Marlboro
Agip
GOODYEAR
sparco

Agip
GOODYEAR
27
J. ALESI
Marlboro
Agip
PIONEER
MAGNETI MARELLI
WEBER
GOODYEAR EAGLE

GOODYEAR
Marlboro
Agip
27
digital
MAGNETI
MARELLI
WEBER
GOODYEAR

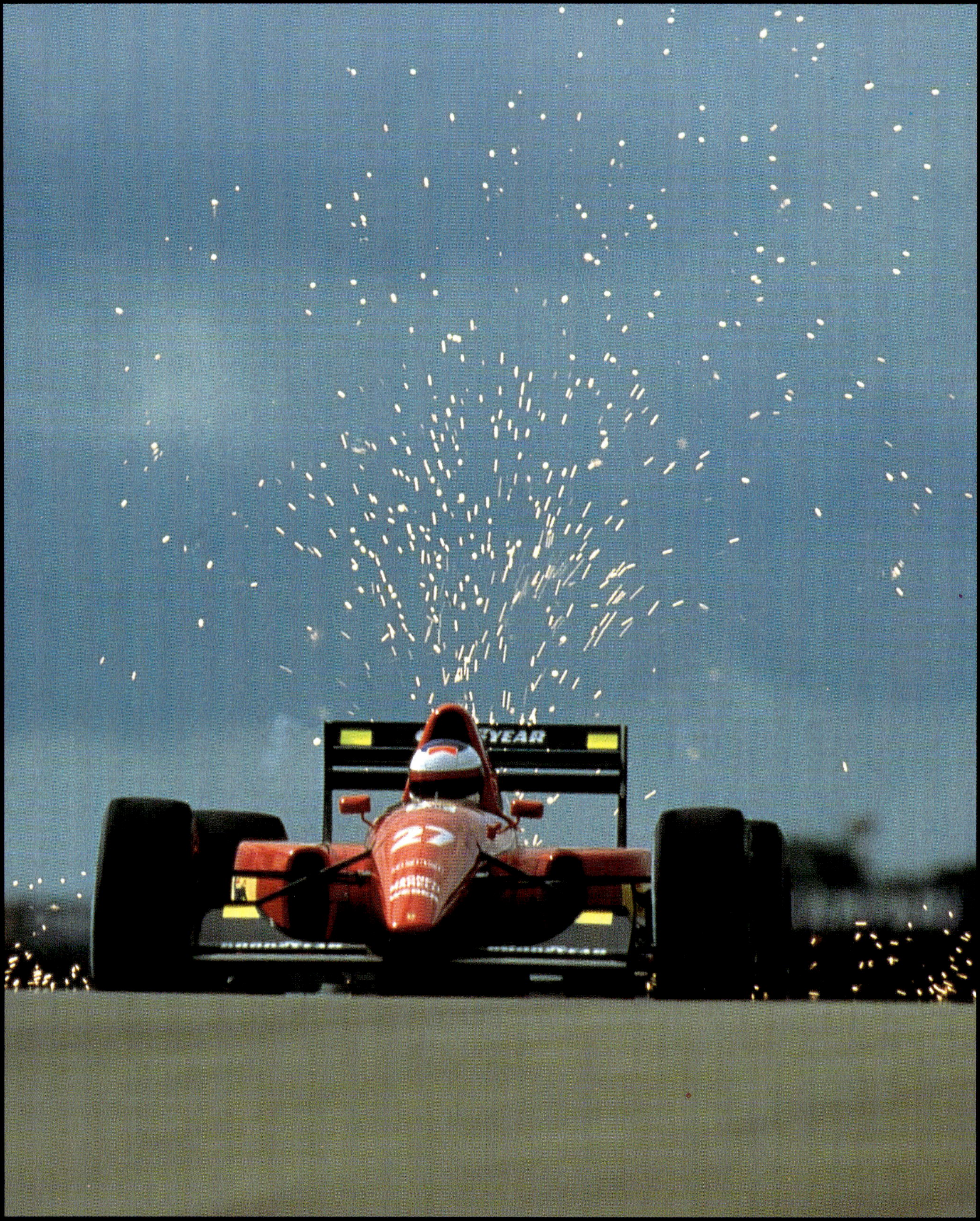
27

# Chapter 6

# *1992, to the Depths of Hell*

If 1991 had been a huge disillusion for Jean, the 1992 season was no improvement, "It was really the worst year," Jose remembers today, "at Ferrari, trust was lost amongst the team, and the directors changed their minds about everything every second day...it was really hard.

For Jean, the 1992 season was an ordeal. Moreover, his co-driver, Ivan Capelli, didn't offer much help – in fact he was let go before the end of the season.

All alone in the task of representing the Scuderia on the track, Jean does what he can. He gets no satisfactory results other than a meager seventh place overall in the championship for his effort. All in all, he mounts the podium twice, but only the third step. "The Ferrari F92A simply wasn't in the same league as its rivals," said Jean at the end of the year, "not only was the chassis impossible to adjust, but it's motor lacked liveliness.

The man from Avignon was equally depressed by results that came only when times didn't count. He openly affirmed that if the season depended on the kilometers raced in private sessions, he was easily the world champion.

During this year, everything went wrong for the Scuderia. Once again, the entire circle of directors had been changed during the winter. Now it was Luca Di Montezemolo, one of Ferrari's ex-directors, who been brought back to pull the reigns. The new bosses can hardly fathom the profundity of the damage done, and can only hope to rectify the situation before Ferrari finds itself in the hinterlands on the F1 rankings.

The situation wasn't improved by the decision to pair a V12 motor, that seemed particularly powerful, with a F92 chassis with a rather original shape, that when combined, however, were unexpectedly inefficient.

At the first Grand Prix event, held at the South African Kyalami circuit, both Ferraris were forced to abandon the race half-way through – both of the cars' oil pumps failed. In Mexico, a few days later, both of the Scuderia's single-seater suffered from a serious lack of power. On the Mexican track's long straight-aways, the Ferraris were never less than 18 km/h slower than the Williams-Renault. "We have two principal problems," Claudio Lombardi, the technical director, remarked at the time, "bad handling, and an insufficient maximum speed."

Which was equivalent to admitting that nothing worked. "In a sense, I'm glad that our problems are so serious," Jean said in an attempt at self-consolation, "because this will incite everyone to get to work to get us past them.

After Mexico, the Ferraris were rushed back to Italy, where they would undergo intensive test driving on the oval at Nardo, that belonged to FIAT. Then the cars were sent directly to Brazil.

The tests aided the discovery of internal problems linked to the motor, for which a jerry-rigged remedy was found before the cars arrived at the Brazilian Grand Prix. Here, both cars would finish in the points.

Then came the Spanish Grand Prix. One of this race's major factors in the rain. As always in such situations, Jean will give one of his driving performances that elucidate his mastery of such conditions, and for which he is famous. After two touches, two spin-outs and a tire-change, he mounts upon the podium's third step. This feat remains one of the greatest examples of bravado in his career.

Starting from the eighth position on the grill, he shoots from the stall, and gains the third position at the first corner. "I was lucky, because my place on the grill was placed right next to a gangway, which meant that my tires were still dry...But I have to admit that we still lack too much top speed to hope to be competitive. Plus, my gear box wouldn't let go into sixth, and had had to stay in fifth on all the straight-aways. That's how Schumacher and Senna easily passed me.

At the end of the race, peddle to the metal and all out, he passed Ivan Capelli and Gerhard Berger, coming in third place. And this in the presence of Luca Di Montezemolo, who, for the first time in his directorship, came to see a race...

This victory sowed hope in the hearts of the tifosi at Imola, where the next event was held. Unfortunately, these renown fans would be sorely disappointed. Jean Alesi and Ivan Capelli had to settle for fourth line on the starting grill. In the final, the Frenchman was forced to forfeit after being hit from behind by Gerhard Berger's McLaren.

In Monaco, Jean qualified for the second line by sheer might, before abandoning the race because of an electrical failure.

The rest of the season didn't go much smoother. At Magny-Cours, after pushing the limits again, in opting for slick tires on the wet track – when all the other drivers had chosen sculpted tires to grip to the slick surface – Jean was once again forced to forfeit.

He'd had just about enough of not being able to vie with the leaders, but he was forced to face and accept the facts: the 1992 season would also be equally hopeless – his Ferrari contract held him back one more year. What to do other than prepare intensely for the 1993 season.

Ferrari had just hired the engineer John Barnard, and counted on him to bring them back to the surface.

# Chapter 7

# *1993, the Slow Recovery*

After the 1992 season, that would take a place in the tifosi's collective memory as a total disaster, 1993 could promise only rectification of Ferrari's situation. However, the corrective measures expected from the engineer, John Bernard, had yet to materialize. Ferrari's season would be, one more time, a deception for all concerned.

None of this stopped Jean Alesi from chalking up a few more exploits on the track. Jean had always loved to pilot his single-seater in a fashion that can't be called anything other than a controlled slide-out. His mastery of this technique was eloquently illustrated by his trials performance at Monza.

In the Grand Prix finals, there will be no sign of Ferrari until the end of the season. The totality of the season's results place Jean barely ahead of Gerhard Berger, who, due to his longtime friendship with the engineer, John Barnard, would become Ferrari's number one driver.

Jean twice climbed the podium in 1993, including an honorable second place won at Monza. But he would also forfeit nine times.

At Ferrari headquarters, the stuation deteriorates further during the 1993 circuit. At the Silverstone, Alesi and Berger are able to secure only twelfth and thirteenth places on the starting grill: their worst results since the year's debut. "The car's steering ability is terrible," Jean explained, "the car jerks on the corners, rather than smoothly changing direction. Moreover, the tires wear out quickly, and the engine still isn't capable of giving 100%." This list of weaknesses seemed irreparable. Jean Todt, whom Luca Di Montezemolo had named as the new head of the Scuderia, could only acknowledge the overwhelming task awaiting him.

At Hockenheim, the following Grand Prix, the Scuderia employed a new motor, with four valves to each cylinder, that showed an improvement over its predecessor on the long straight-aways of Hockenheim track. Alas, the improvement was nearly imperceptible in the race results: Jean finished seventh overall after having fought like a bat out of hell.

The Scuderia's recovery wouldn't become tangible until the end of August, at the events in Belgium, then at Monza.

At Ferrari, however, nobody was too concerned with the events taking place on the tracks. From the start, the crew was looking beyond, to the 1994 season. The engineers had totally dedicated themselves to the new car – entirely redesigned by John Barnard – that would come out for the 1994 circuit.

In spite of the continuing difficulties the Scuderia faced, , Jean decided to extend his contact with Ferrari two more years, "I'd worked so hard for the last three years, I didn't want to

67

leave my place so that someone else comes along and benefits from my travails. With Jean Todt at the helm and John Barnard at the design table, I was quite certain that Ferrari would be capable of producing results in 1994. In 1992, before Luca Di Montezemolo came to us, people were always leaving Ferrari. And those who stayed were in constant terror of being let go...When Di Montezemolo hired Jean Todt, everything got a little better. Todt told us that he needed everyone in order to win, and that it would be a huge task to get us to that point. Since that day, there's no one who doesn't give it his all wholeheartedly...

For the coming 1994 season, in consideration of his results, Jean succeeded to negotiate an equal treatment with Gerhard Berger, who would no longer be the first-position driver. Just one more reason for the man from Avignon to feel confident...

# Chapter 8 — *1994, Hope's Coming*

Finally! After four years in the dark, la Scuderia Ferrari found itself in the spotlight of victory again. However, even if Gerhard Berger would bring home the German Grand Prix title, he would also admit that the Scuderia's single-seaters didn't fill the top grill positions as often as the directors had promised at the start of the year.

Unfortunately, from the first Grand Prix of the year, it became altogether evident: even though the 412T1 was certainly a very attractive car, it was a complete failure at a technical level. It's the victim of a default that won't be corrected until the French Grand Prix. On the other hand, the new titanium gear box and flat underside provide the car with a positive edge.

For Jean personally, the start of the 1994 season was catastrophic. Just after the first Grand Prix, he'd had a terrible accident in the private sessions, on the Mugello circuit, that would keep him from taking part in the Pacific Grand Prix, and that of Saint-Marin. After the accident, that happened at 200 km/h, he would momentarily lose movement in his left arm. He'll wear a back-brace until the fifth, sixth and seventh vertebras he'd crushed had healed.

Upon being brought to Paris to be examined, Professor Gerard Saillant, a specialist in sports auto accidents, finds that Jean has healed very quickly, but risks complications if he gets behind the wheel before the Grand Prix in Monaco. He was replaced by Nicola Larini for the next two events.

For his return to the track, at Monaco, Jean is unlucky in hitting David Brabham's Simtek in the race, and loses his nose piece. After a good minute in the pits to fix it, he has no chance for a spot on the podium; but he'll still earn two points by finishing in fifth place. Gerhard Berger, his teammate, comes in third in the Monaco event, and uses the opportunity to complain about the problems at Ferrari, "You've got to admit that our chassis doesn't work," he declares, "we understand what the basic problem is, and I think we need to find a way to fix it. In the meantime, we're all suffering...

Yet, in Canada, the Scuderia shocks all, when Jean Alesi qualifies for the first line. In the final, he finished third, without being able to fairly dispute the race with the leaders.

But it was really during the English Grand Prix that Ferrari assumes a position amongst the top teams. From the practice sessions, the two cars merit a place in the second line from the starting grill. For the first time, Berger uses the new 043 qualification motor. In the race, Jean Alesi finishes second, without being very satisfied with his machine, "I'm looking forward to Hockenheim," he said, "because all you need there is a strong motor, and ours is really powerful right now.

Once arrived at Hockenheim, the two

Ferraris will find themselves both on the first line. Gerhard Berger took the pole position, but Jean didn't have a chance to defend himself: as the Frenchman hurled himself into the last fast lap, his hood flew off in the middle of the straight-away. He slowed to a stop in the pits to reattach the piece, when his pressure pump comes off in its turn. There's too much work to do and too little time to try to get back into the trials race.

In the final, Jean didn't go very far. He abandons the race after only half a lap due to engine failure. Contrarily, Berger takes home the victory that the Scuderia awaited since the Spanish Grand Prix, 1990.

Two weeks later, in Hungary, everything was different. After the sessions with a car Jean had decided was simply not fit to race, he landed only thirteenth place on the starting grill. This was the beginning of a catastrophe that wouldn't better itself in the race, for Jean would withdraw from the race when his hydraulic system breaks down. This was a shame, because up to that point, Jean had succeeded in making a come-back that was interrupted only by this mechanical problem.

In Spa, Jean was back in good spirits. But this wasn't to last long: out of the stalls like a rocket, he moved ahead to second place, reaching the leader, Michael Schumacher, only to abandon in the third lap, "What can I say?" Jean remarks upon his return to the stands, "one more time, the car was excellent, and once more, I'm unlucky. It's always me who runs into problems..." Thus, he leaves on vacation, coming back two weeks later, and raring to go. He arrives at the Italian Grand Prix, and begins a week that he'll long remember.

In the trials, he'll take the pole-position for the first time in his career, "My last poles were in my Formula 3000 days with Eddie Jordan," Jean remembers, "Sure I'm happy: it's a big day for me. But mostly, I'm thinking about the race tomorrow, because I'm not really confident in the dependability of my car. We've improved every aspect; it's not undriveable like it was before. I'd even say it's a really good car...

In the final, Jean was ready for a win, supported by the crowd of tifosi. However, a rupture in the transmission during the pit stop will dash his hopes for victory. Jean jumps out of his car, throws his gloves down on the ground and walked off the circuit. "He wouldn't speak to anybody at all for two days," Jose recalls. At such a point, it was no longer bad luck, but a veritable curse that kept the Frenchman from taking his first title.

Things don't get any better in Portugal, at the following Grand Prix event. Jean was in third position, and took a try at David Brabham's Simtek, when Brabham, out of the blue, rammed the Ferrari. "It was too bad, because everything was working well," Jean regretted, "and because I'm sure that no one could've taken third place from me.

In Japan, Jean takes third place again, after a superb duel with Nigel Mansell. "I'm really happy with this result, even if Mansell wore me out with his continual attacks. I should have stayed concentrated, without letting go for one second. I've got to admit, he still has it in him, for an old guy.

Jean would finish the 1994 season on a sixth place taken at the Australian Grand Prix. "I had too much bad luck this year. I've got to turn the page as fast as possible, and start thinking about 1995...

For, again, Ferrari's directors promised the moon for the coming season...

# Photo legends

| | | | | |
|---|---|---|---|---|
| Page 73 | Deep in thought, Spanish Grand Prix, Barcelona, 1994. | | bottom | The podium, Italian Grand Prix, Monza, 1993. |
| Page 74 | Brazilian Grand Prix, Interlagos, 1993. | Page 84 | left | With his loyal confident, Jose. If there's a problem, it's his older brother Jean turns to. |
| Page 75 | Monaco Grand Prix, 1994. | | | |
| Page 76-77 | Lost in the crowd, 1993. | | middle | A moment of relaxation in the pool. |
| Page 78 top | Monaco's magnificent course, 1994. | | right | On a motorcycle, the easiest way to get from the track to the hotel. French Grand Prix, Magny-Cours, 1993. |
| bottom | In front of Michael Schumacher, Monaco Grand Prix, 1993. | | | |
| Page 79 top | Out of the race at Imola. Saint-Marin Grand Prix, 1993. | Page 85 top | | "What will these journalists dream up next?" Jean reads the paper at the end of a day of trials. |
| bottom | A two-armed salute for the crowd. Italian Grand Prix, Monza, 1993. | | bottom | With his mother, on his wedding day, June 21, 1992. |
| Page 80 top | Jean lives through a series of forfeits; his bad luck is remarkable in it's regularity. Saint-Marin Grand Prix, Imola, 1993. | Page 86 top | | As if the F1 wasn't thrilling enough...or, a moment of pleasure with the Air Brigades. |
| middle | Abandoning at the Spanish Grand Prix, Barcelona, 1992. | | bottom | With his masseur, Pierre Baleydier. Due to the muscular strain F1 driving demands, a massage session is necessary after each day of practice. |
| bottom | Repeat performance at the Belgian Grand Prix, Spa, 1994. | Page 87 | | Monaco Grand Prix, 1993. |
| Page 81 | One of the people who have made Jean a legend. German Grand Prix, Hockenheim, 1993. | Page 88 | | A bit optimistic coming out of a turn. Belgian Grand Prix, Spa, 1994. |
| Page 82 | In action. Saint-Marin Grand Prix, Imola, 1993. | Page 89 | | Back-lit in a season not filled with light. Portuguese Grand Prix, Estoril, 1994. |
| | | Page 90 | | Hide and seek amongst the trees. |
| Page 83 top | With Niki Lauda, hired in 1992 as an outside consultant by Ferrari's president, Luca Di Montazemolo. | Page 91 | | A pit stop at Ferrari. |
| | | Page 92 top | | "VVrrrrooooom," Jean likes driving so much that he has to make believe between two trials sessions. |
| middle | With Jean Todt. | | | |

# Photo legends

| | | |
|---|---|---|
| | bottom | With Gerhard Berger in the stands, after having clocked two first line times. German Grand Prix, Hockenheim, 1994. |
| Page 93 | | In the privacy of the stalls. European Grand Prix, 1994. |
| Page 94 | | With Gerhard Berger, standing on the wall of the stalls after his first pole-position. Italian Grand Prix, Monza, 1994. |
| Page 95 | top | Escorted by the carabinieri after having taken his first pole-position. Italian Grand Prix, Monza, 1994. |
| | bottom | In action in an Italian Grand Prix that will end badly for Jean. Monza, 1994. |
| Page 96 | | The start at the Italian Grand Prix. Jean uses his pole-position to his utmost advantage to take the lead, leaving the crowd and confusion behind, 1994. |
| Page 97 | | The blessed day. Canadian Grand Prix, Montreal, 1994. |
| Page 98 | top | In action, Italian Grand Prix, Monza, 1994. |
| | bottom | The Mirabeau corner in back-lighting, Monaco Grand Prix, 1994. |
| Page 99 | | In action. Italian Grand Prix, Monza, 1994. |
| Page 100 | | A lack of definition in Monaco, 1993. |
| Page 101 | | In action. Italian Grand Prix, Monza, 1994. |
| Page 102 | top | At the starting grill, with father Franck and Jean Todt. Hungarian Grand Prix, Budapest, 1994. |
| | bottom | A bird's-eye view of Monaco. |

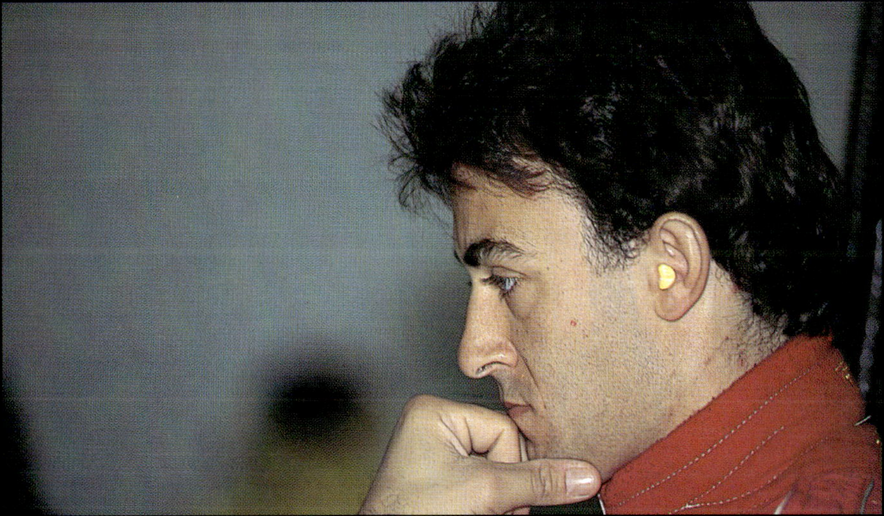

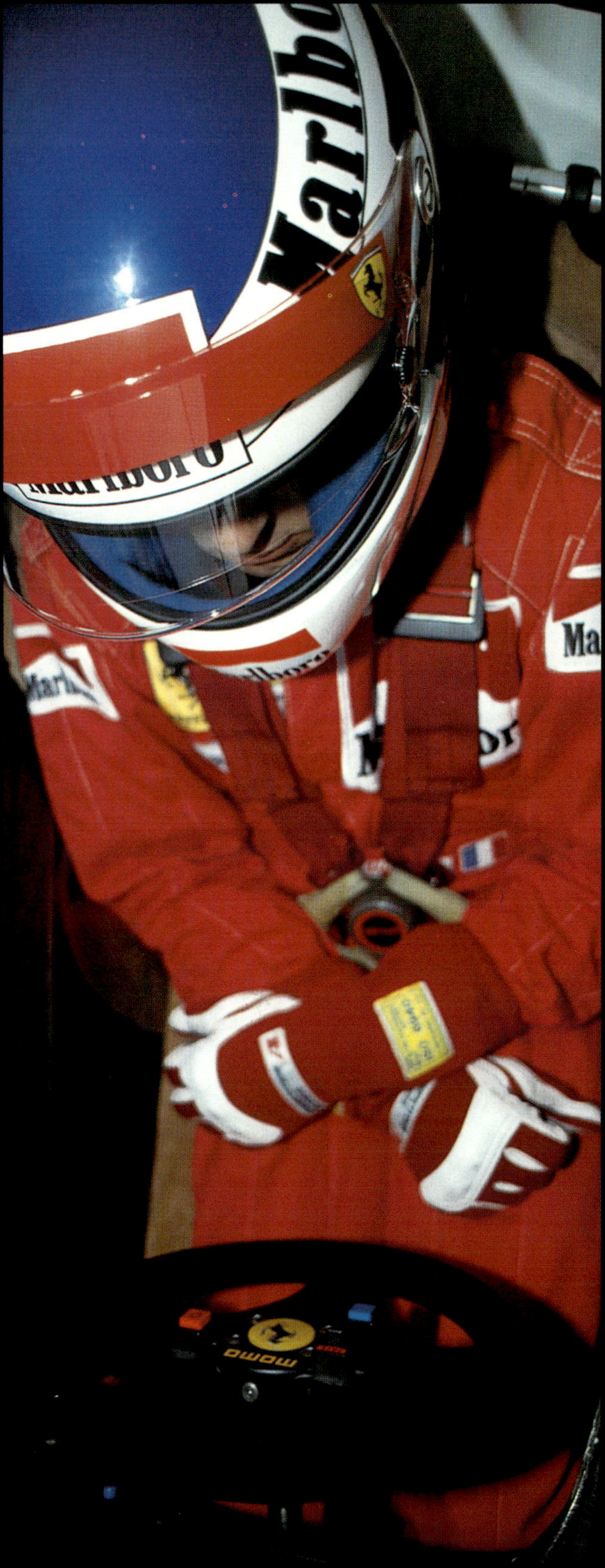
Marlboro
momo

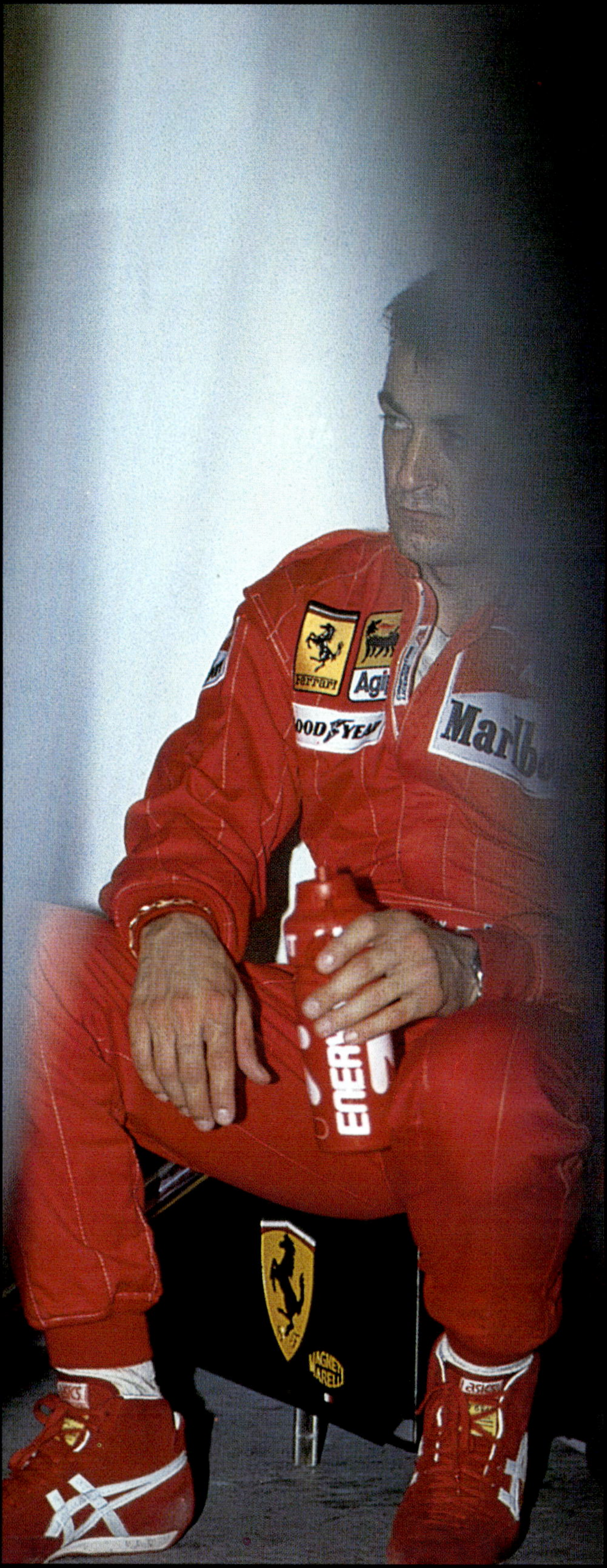
Ferrari
MAGNETI MARELLI

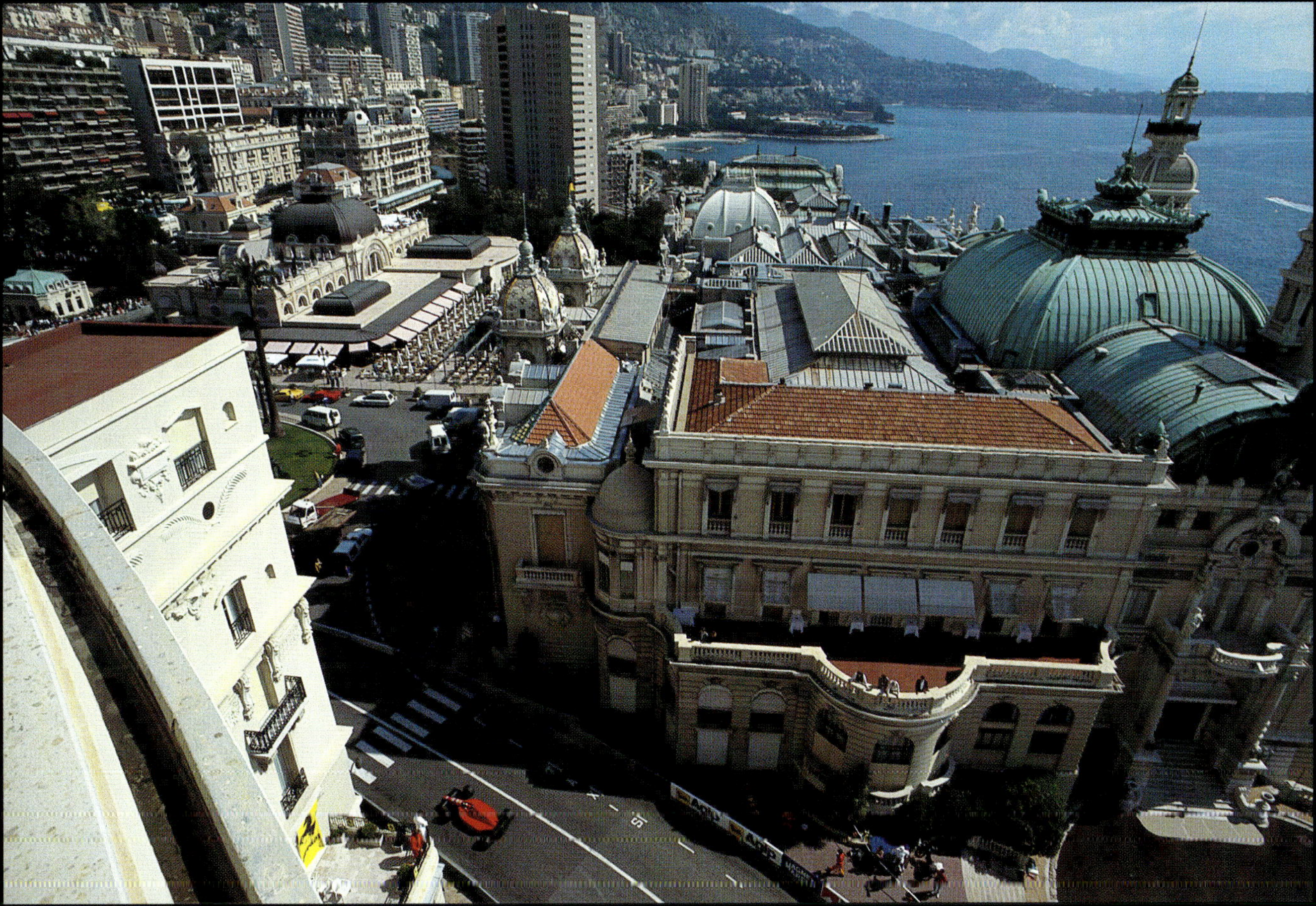

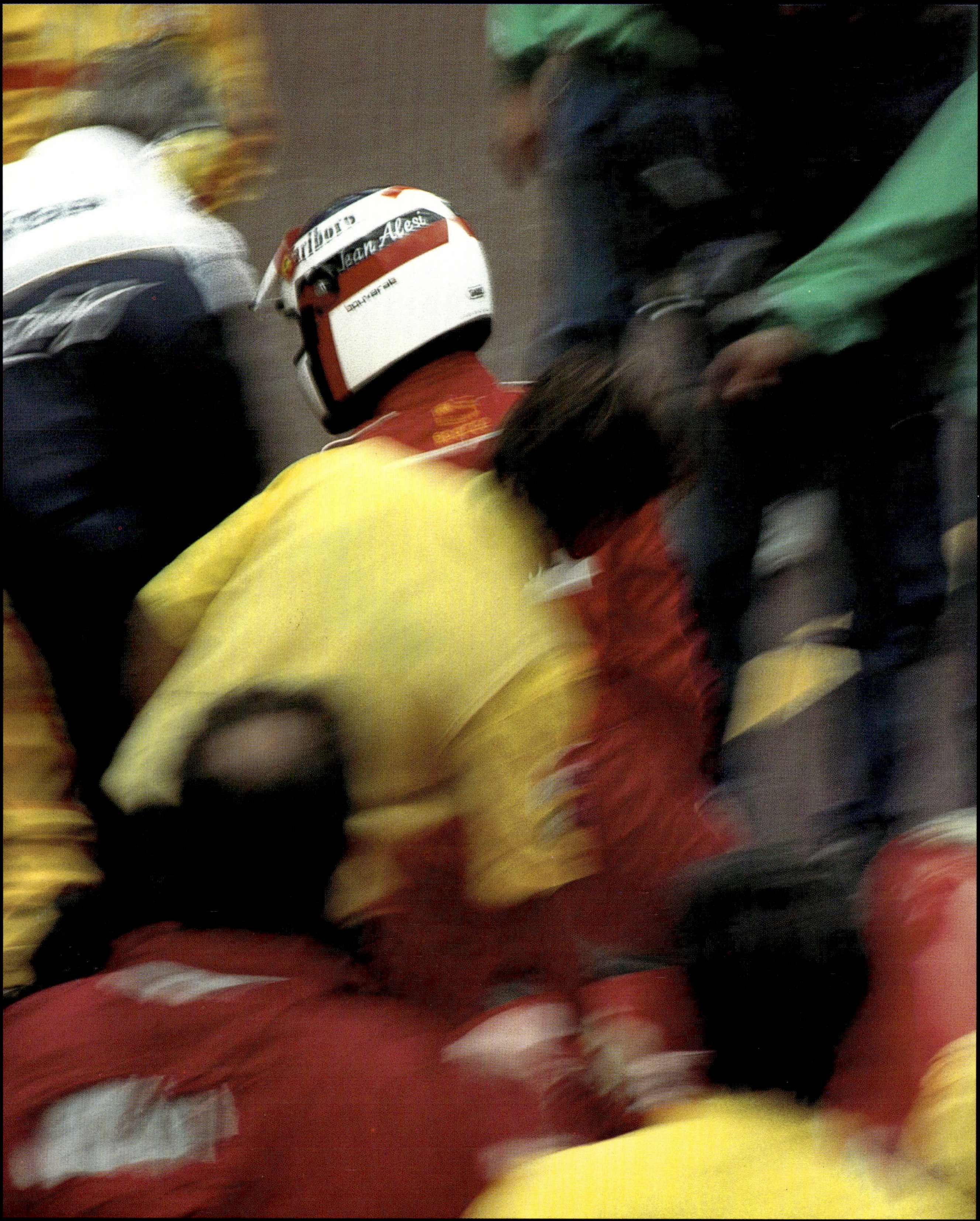
Jean Alesi

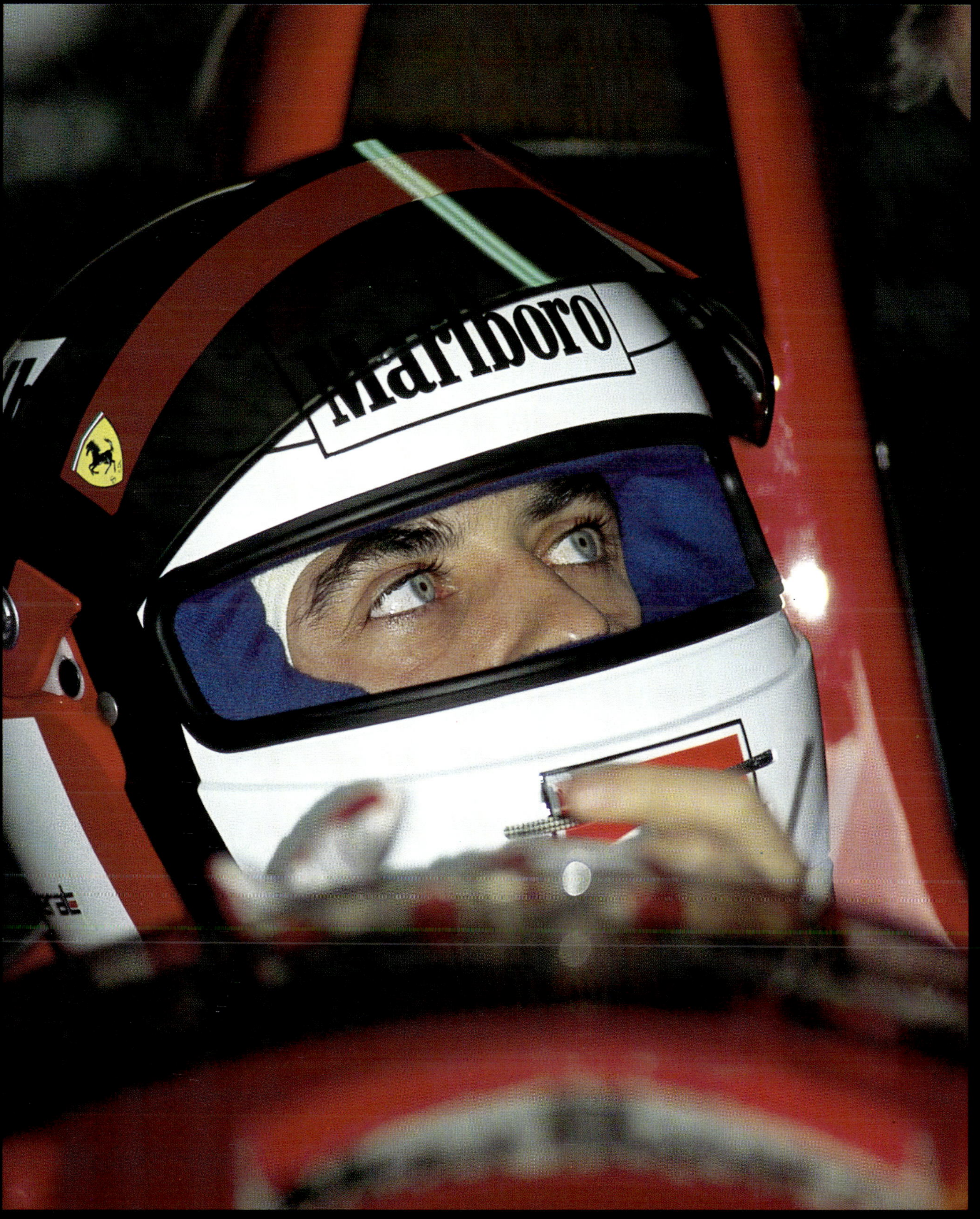
Marlboro

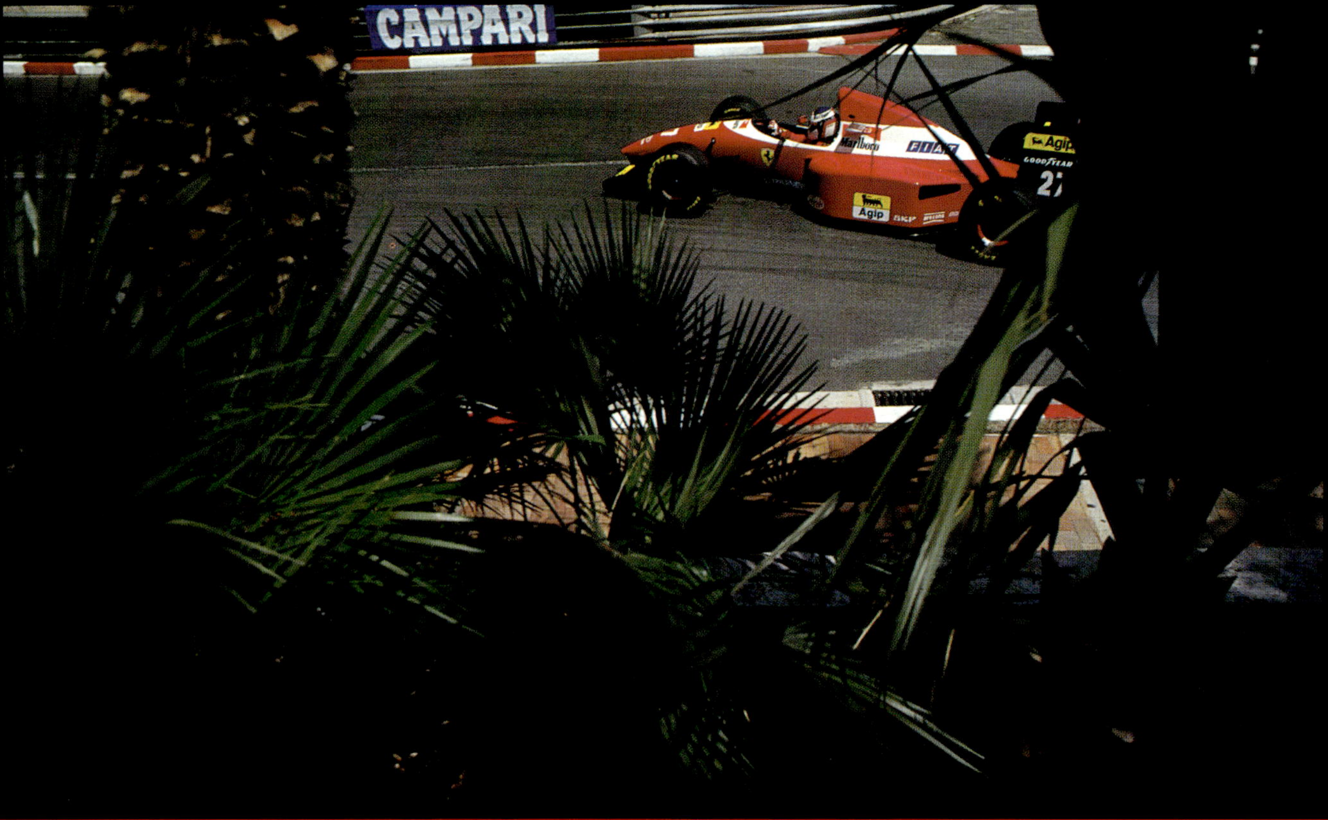
CAMPARI
Agip

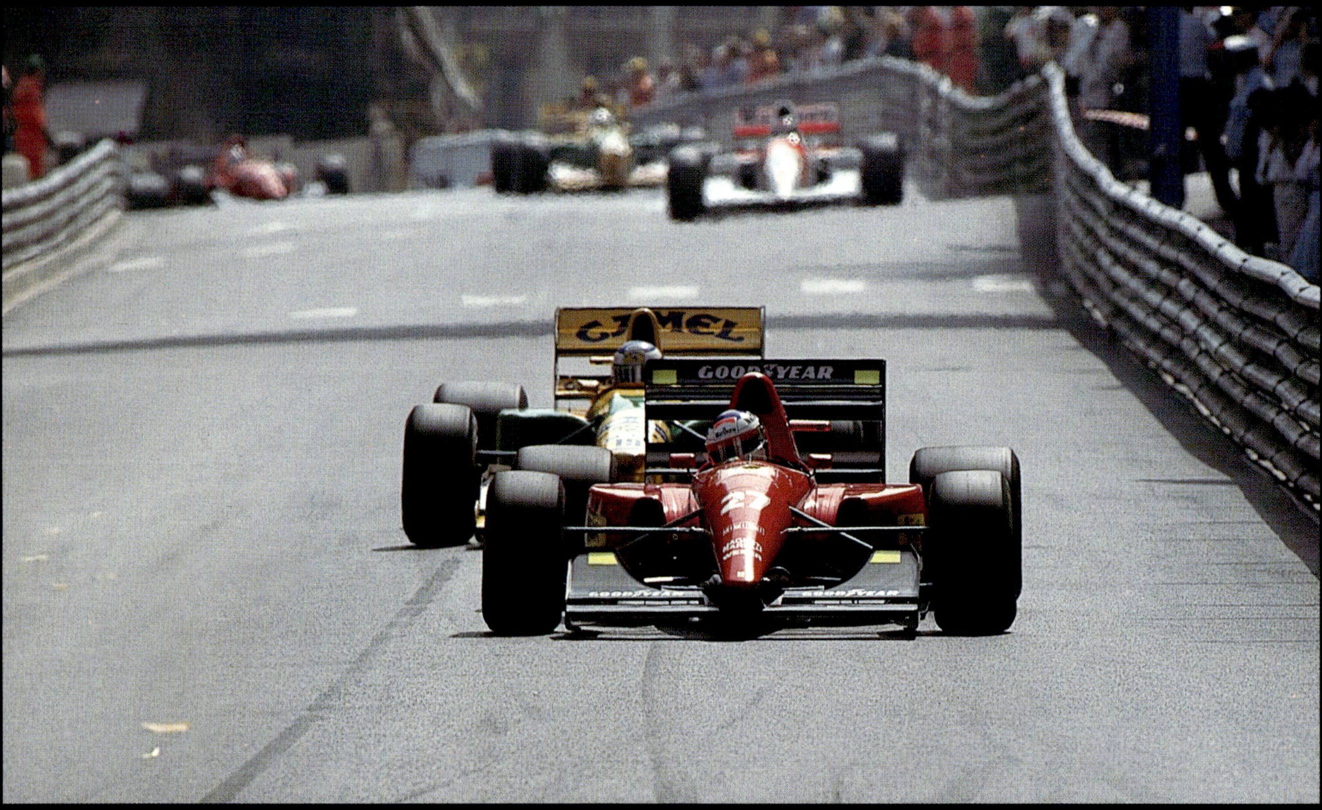
GOODYEAR

Epoxytecnica
VIA MALPIGHI 25 - FAENZA

Marlboro
FIAT
PIONEER
Agip
Agip
27

Agip
GOODYEAR
28
FIAT
J. ALESI
Marlboro
Agip

J. ALESI
Marlboro
FIAT
Agip
GOODYEAR
28
GOODYEAR
EAGLE
Agip
MAGNETI MARELLI
WEBER
arexons
SKF

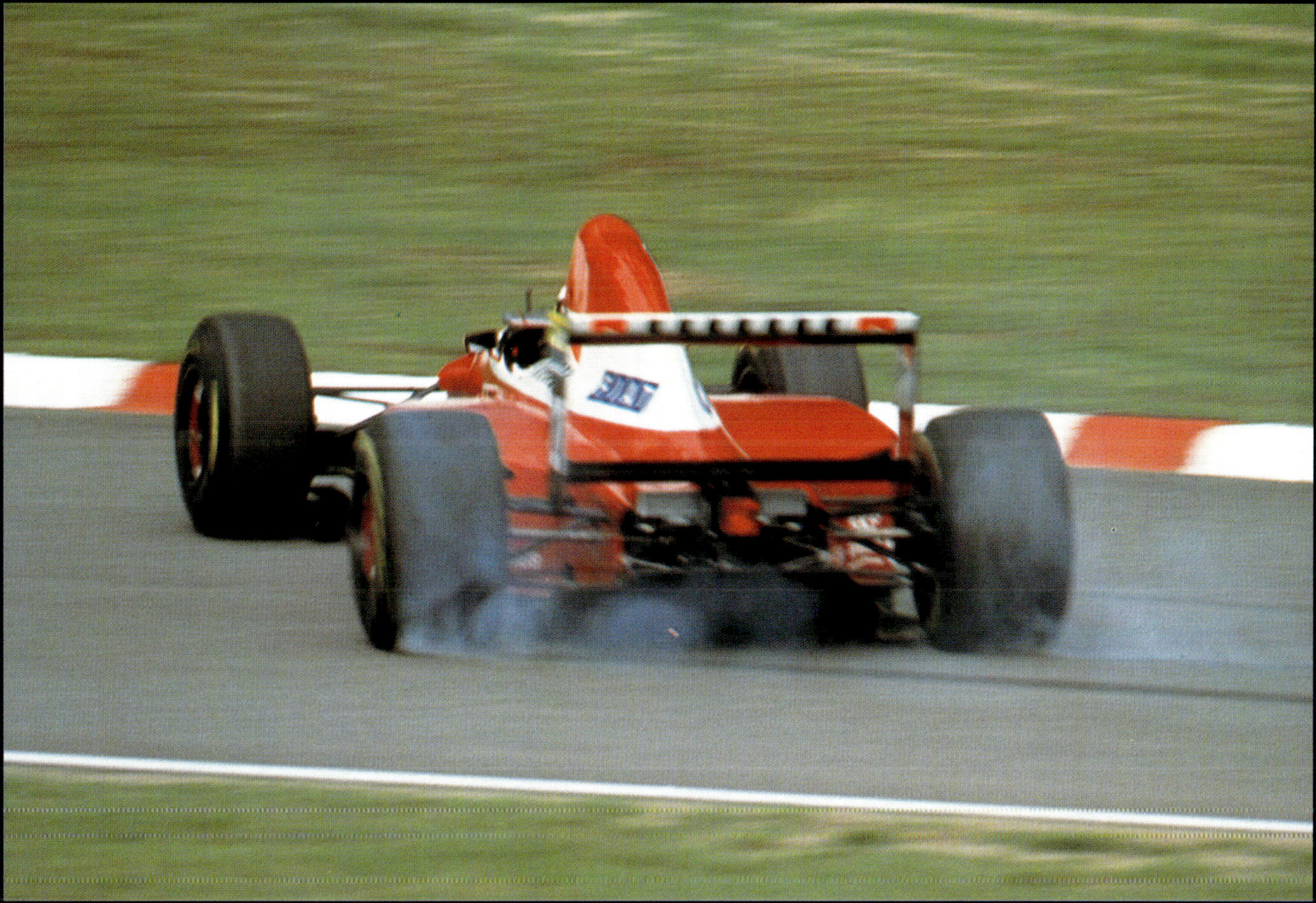

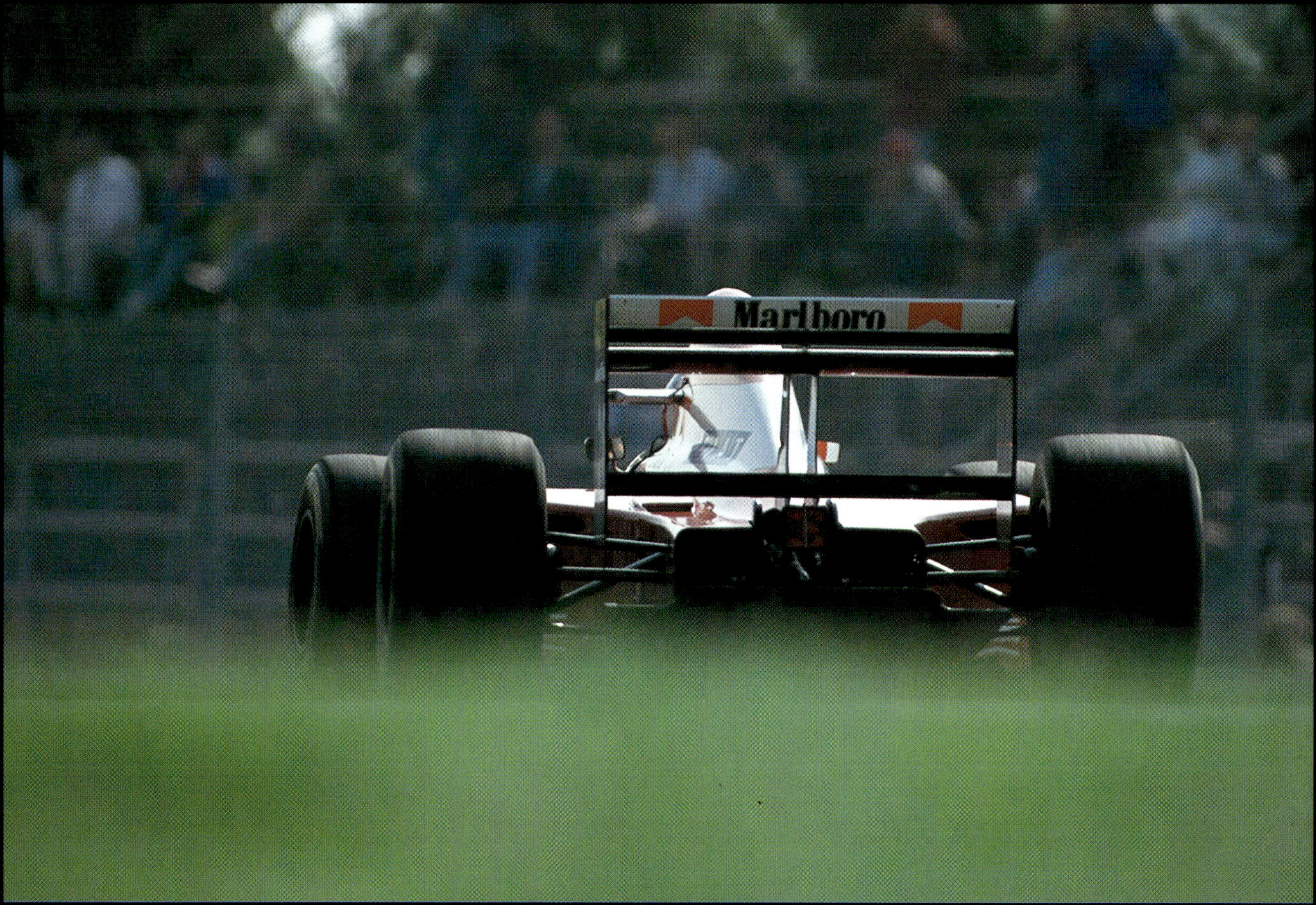
Marlboro

J. ALESI
Agip

Marlboro
Agip
GOODYEAR
Marlboro

UNO
IAT
PIONEER
FORMULA 1
REMIO

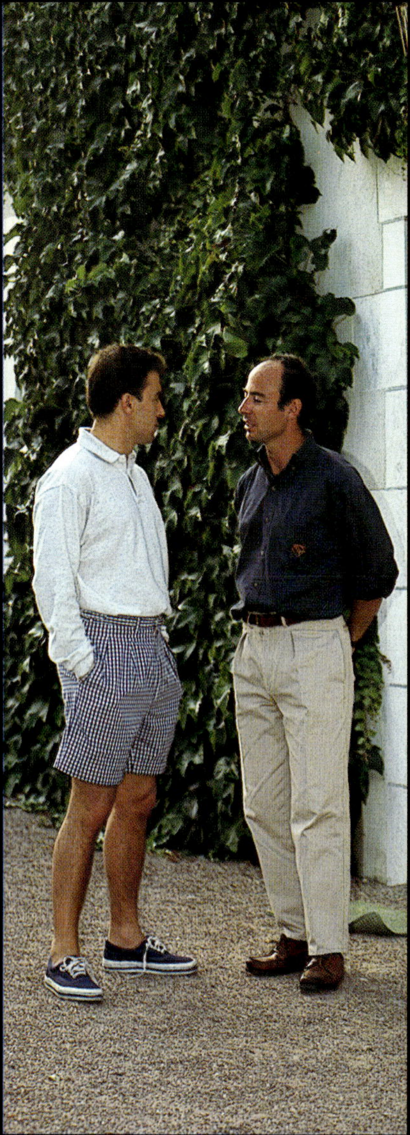

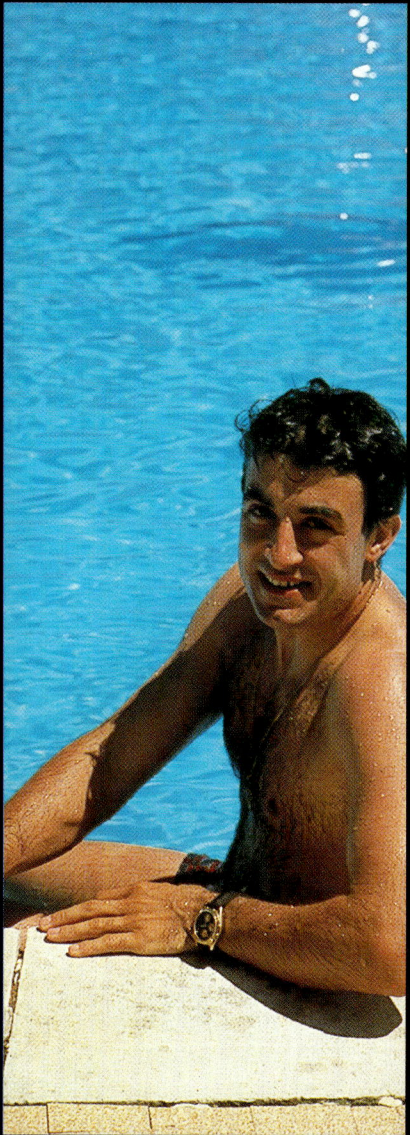

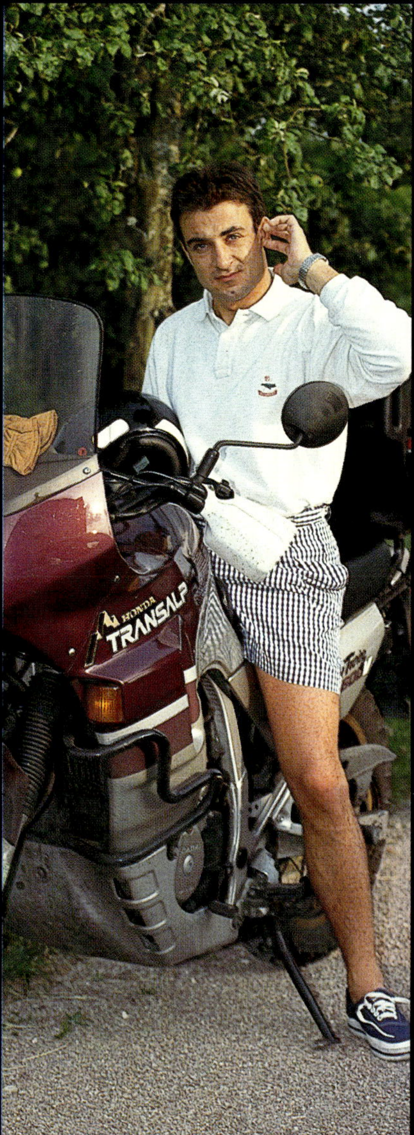
HONDA
TRANSALP

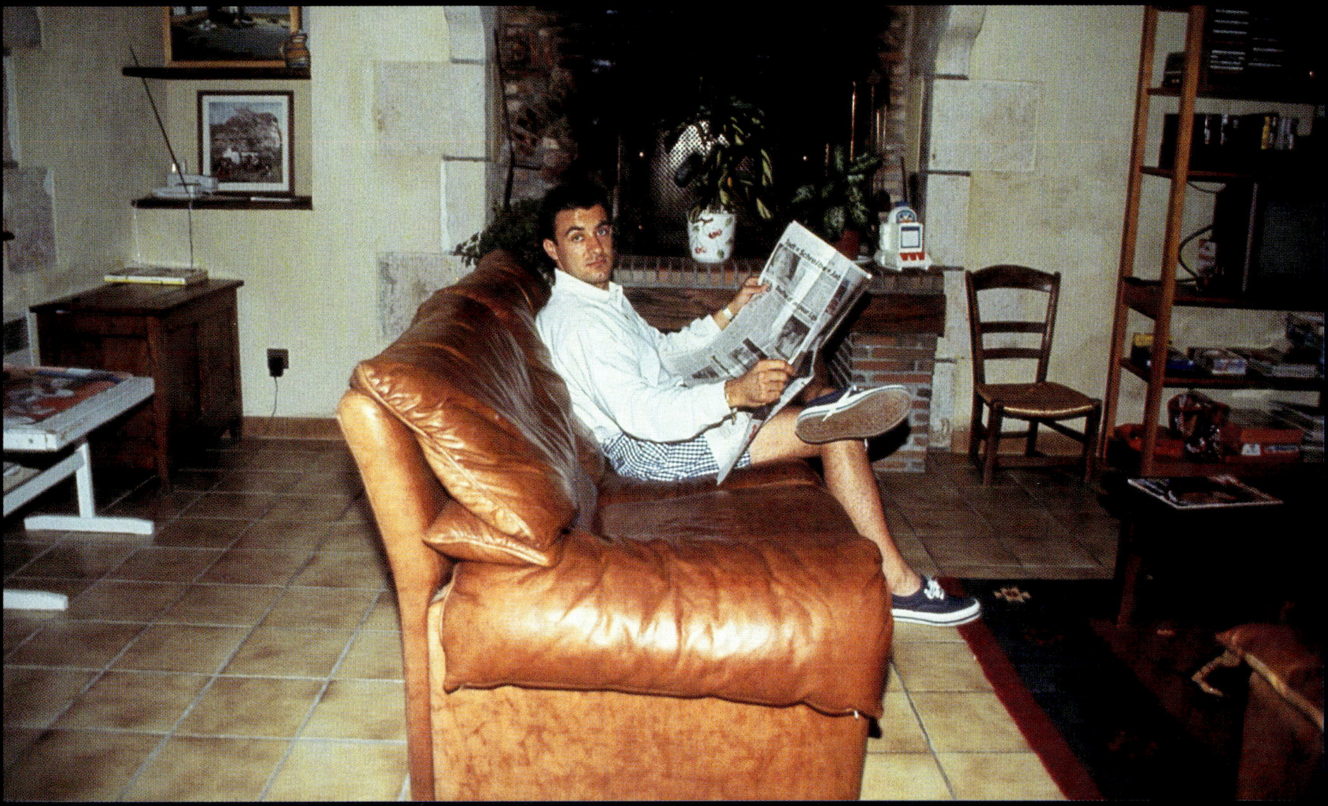

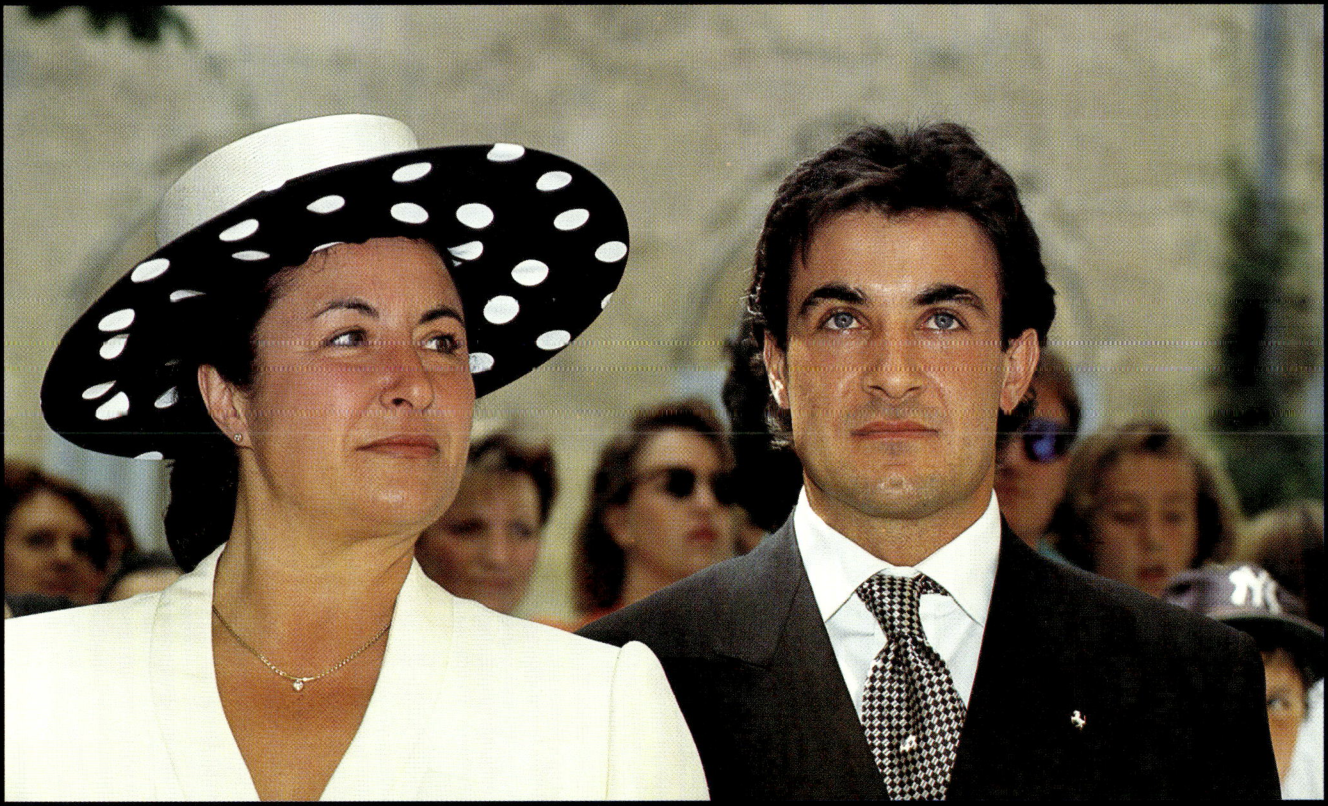

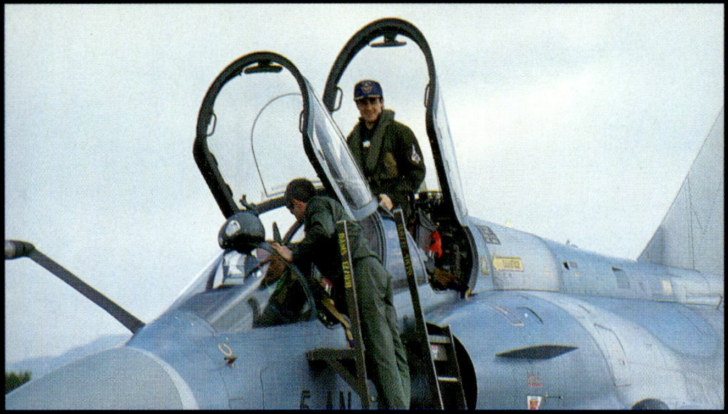

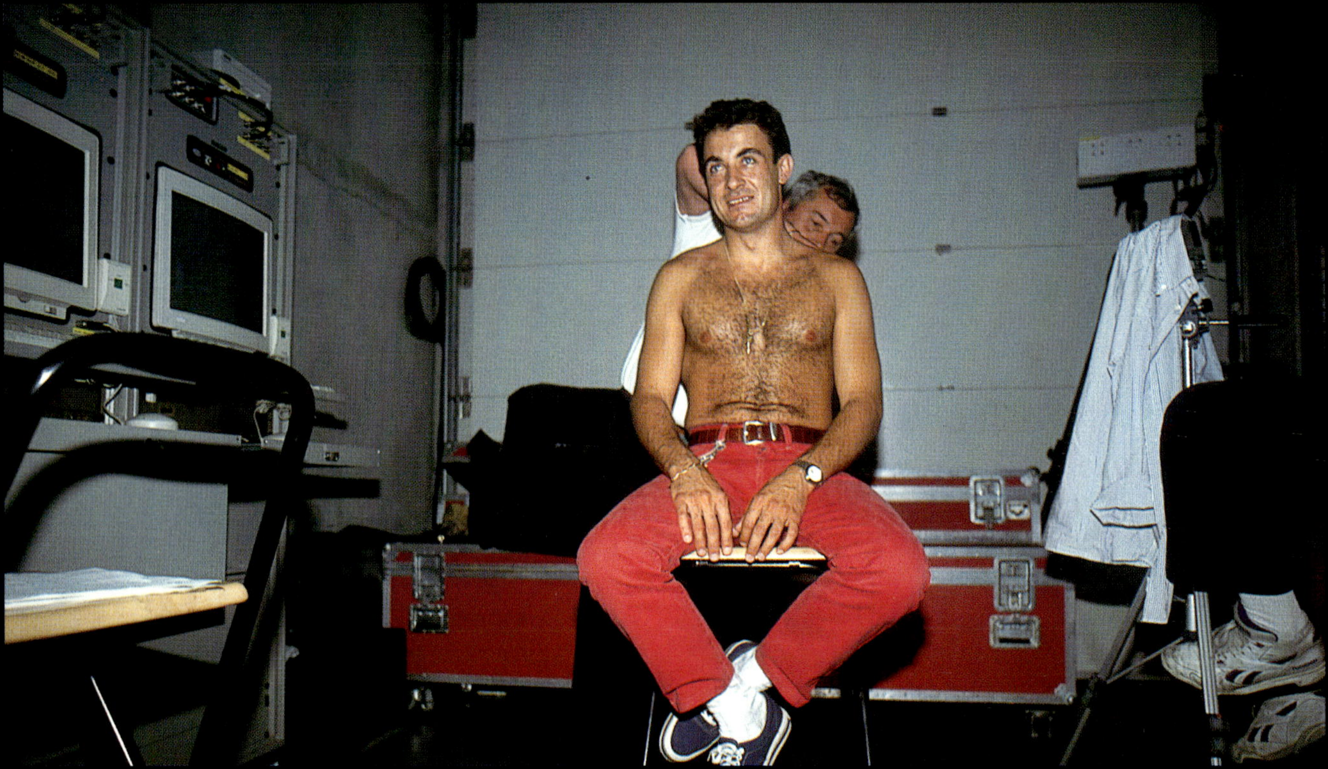

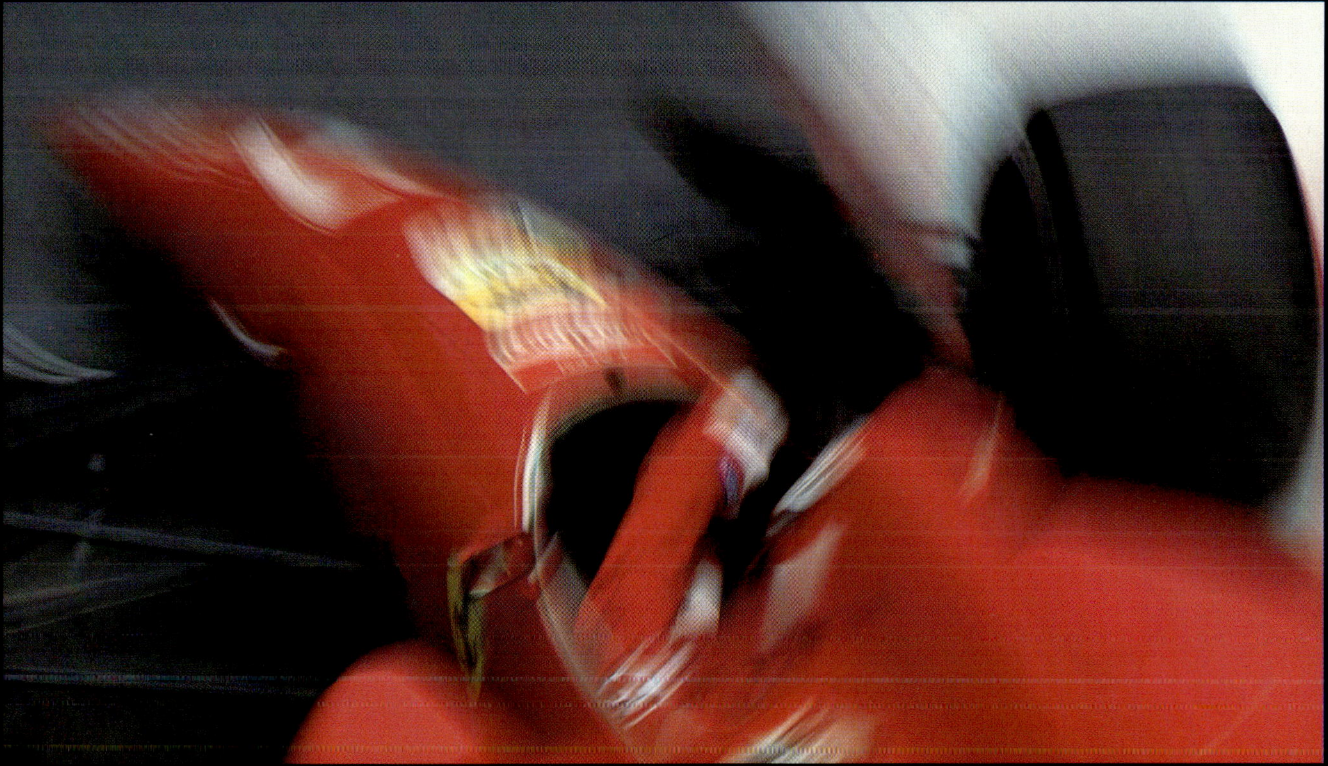

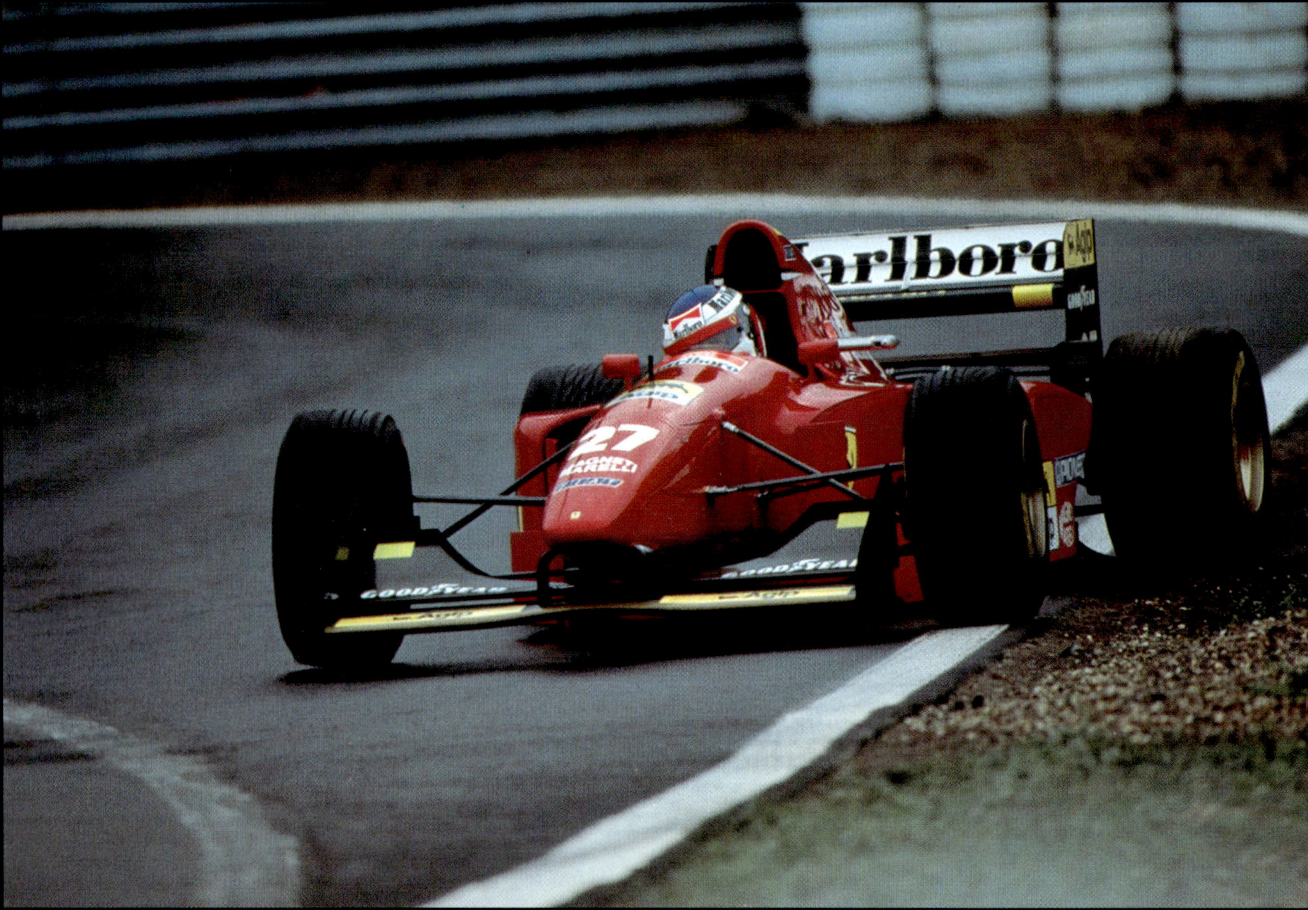
arlboro
Agip
27
GOODYEAR

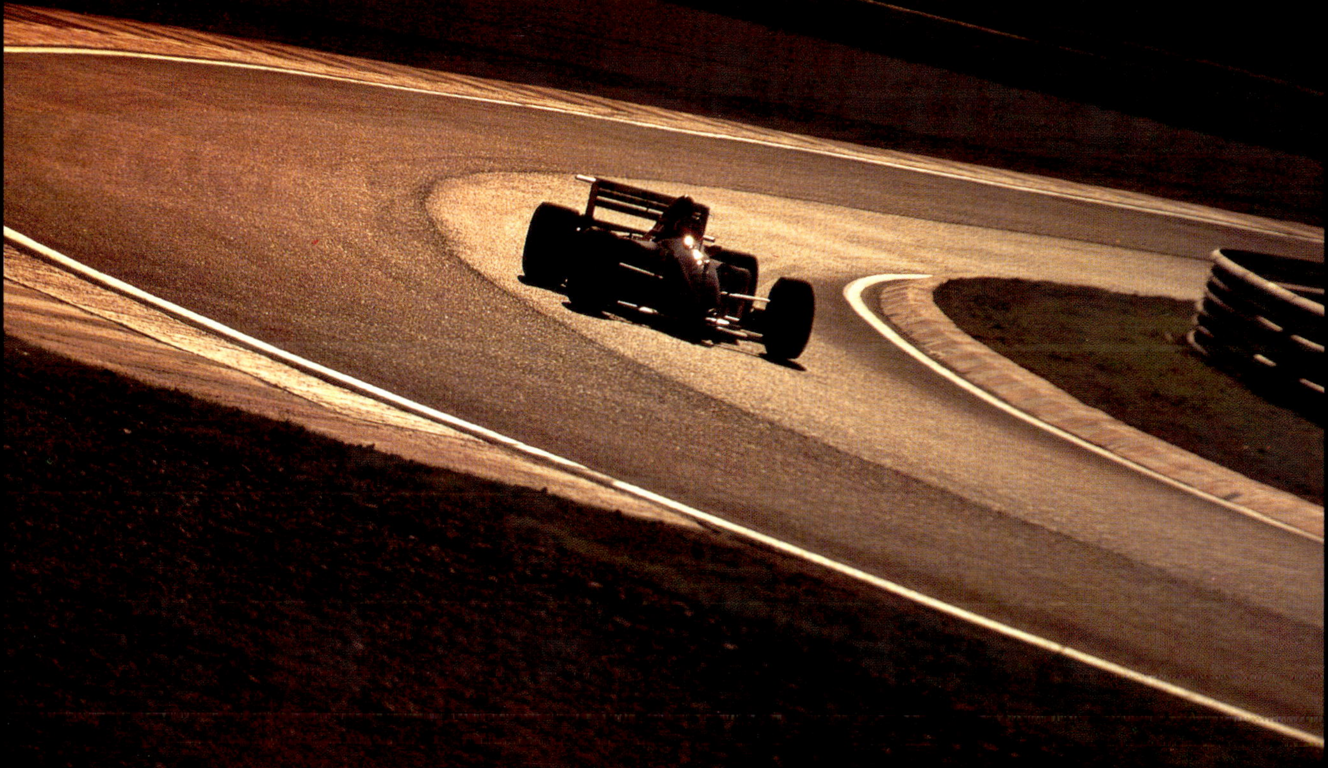

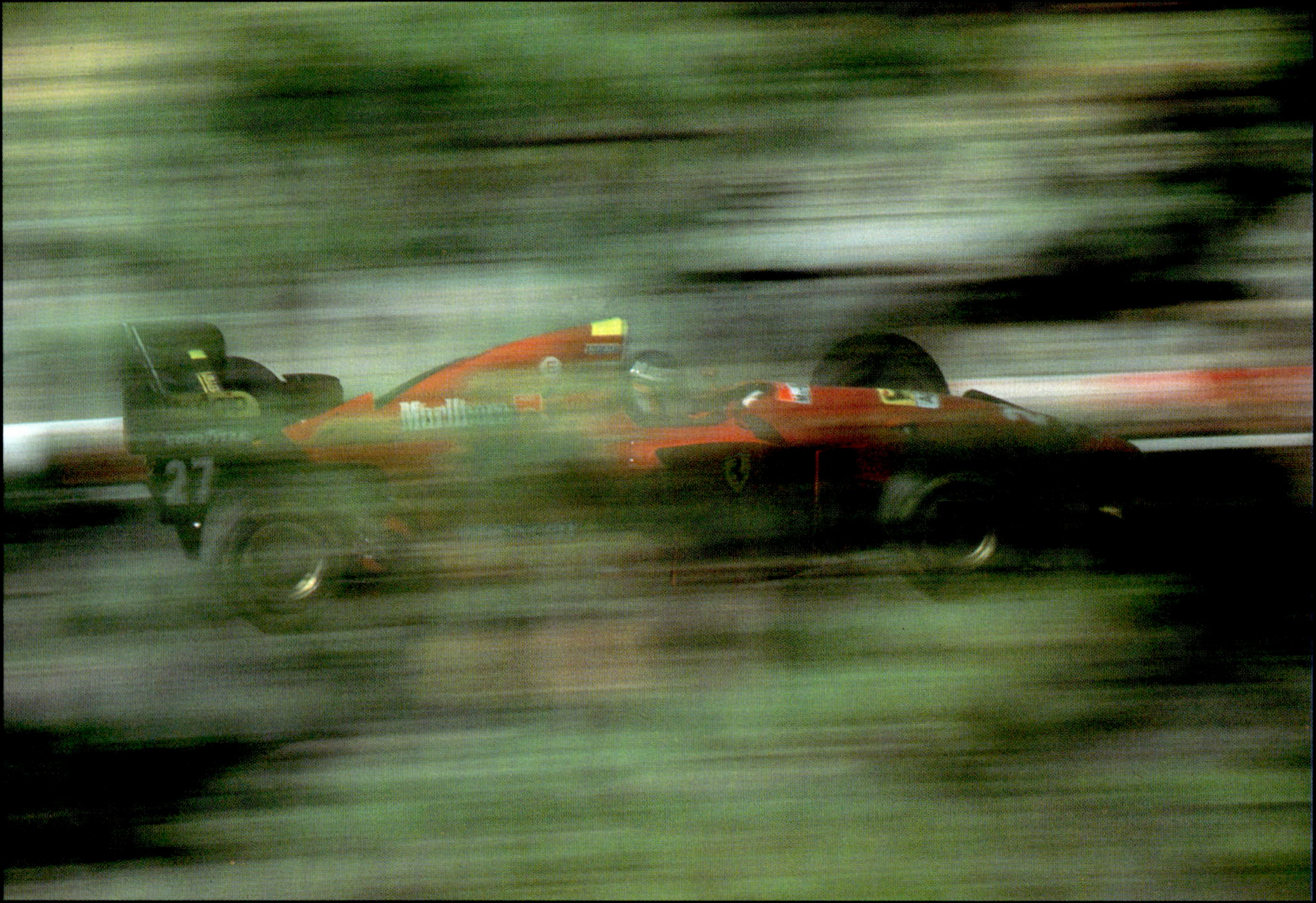
27

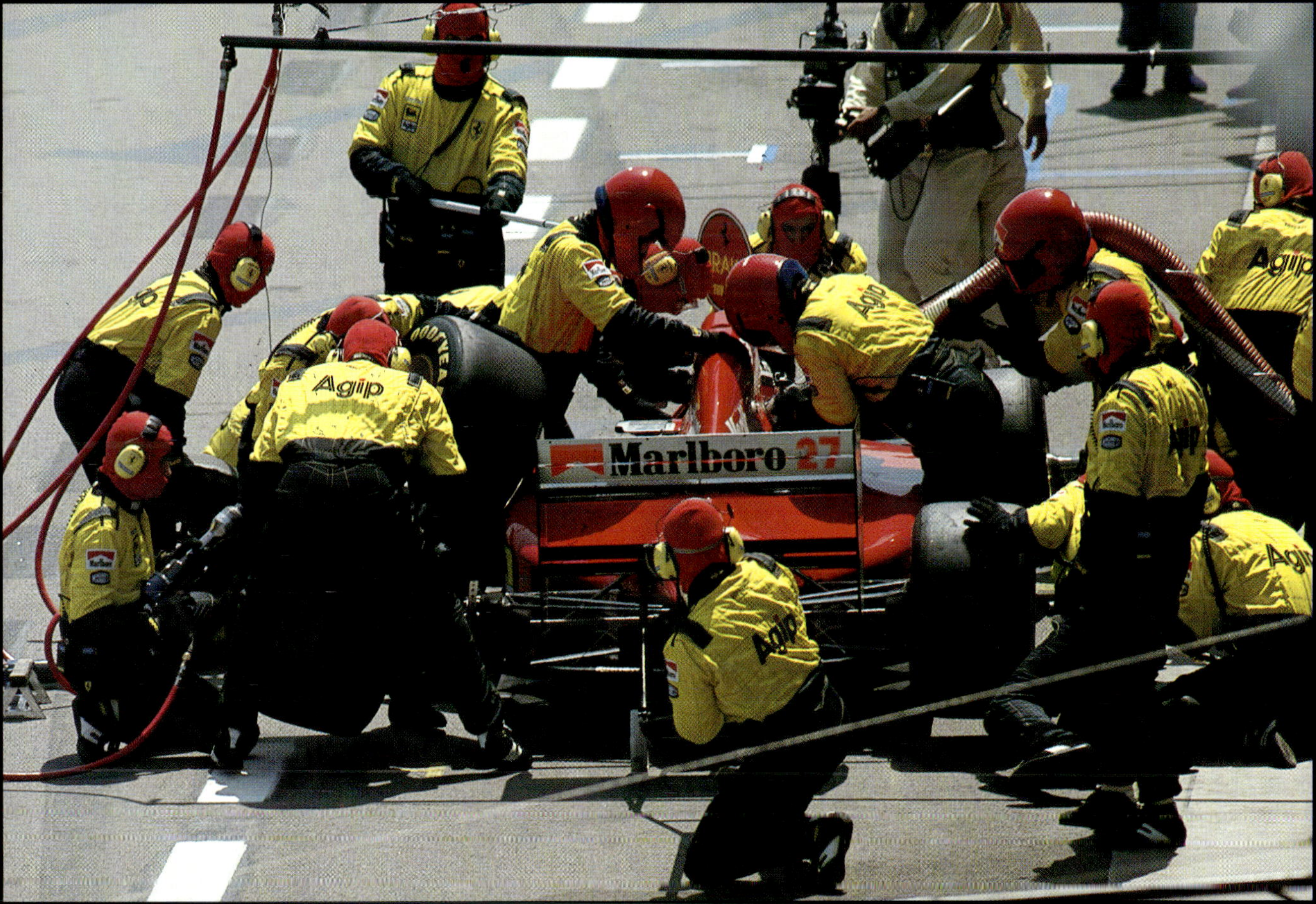
Marlboro 27
Agip
Agip
Agip
Agip
Agip

sparco
J.Alesi

G. BERGE
WORLD CHAMPION TEAM
Ferrari
Agip
GOODYEAR
WORLD CHAMPIONSHIP TEAM

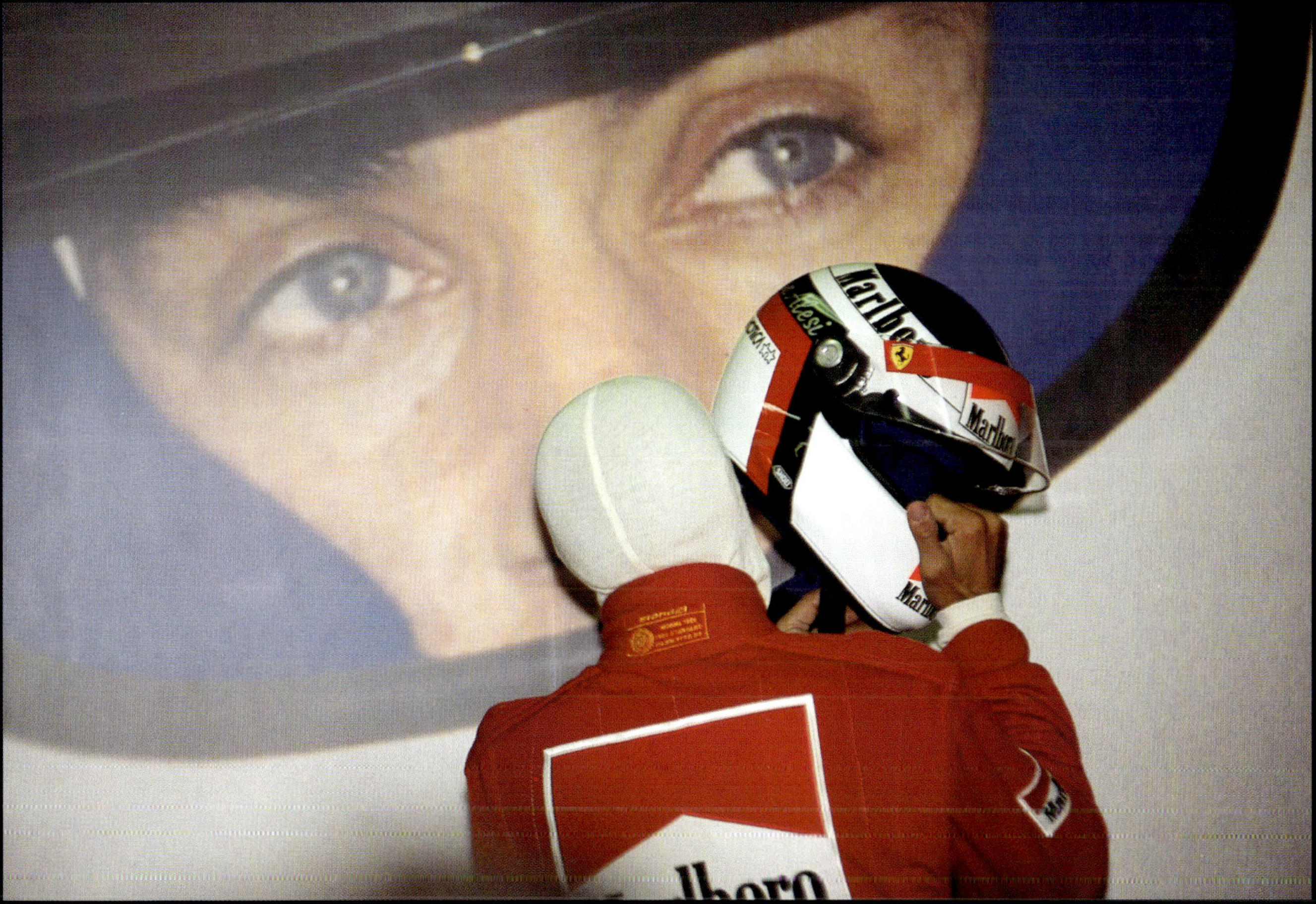
Marlboro

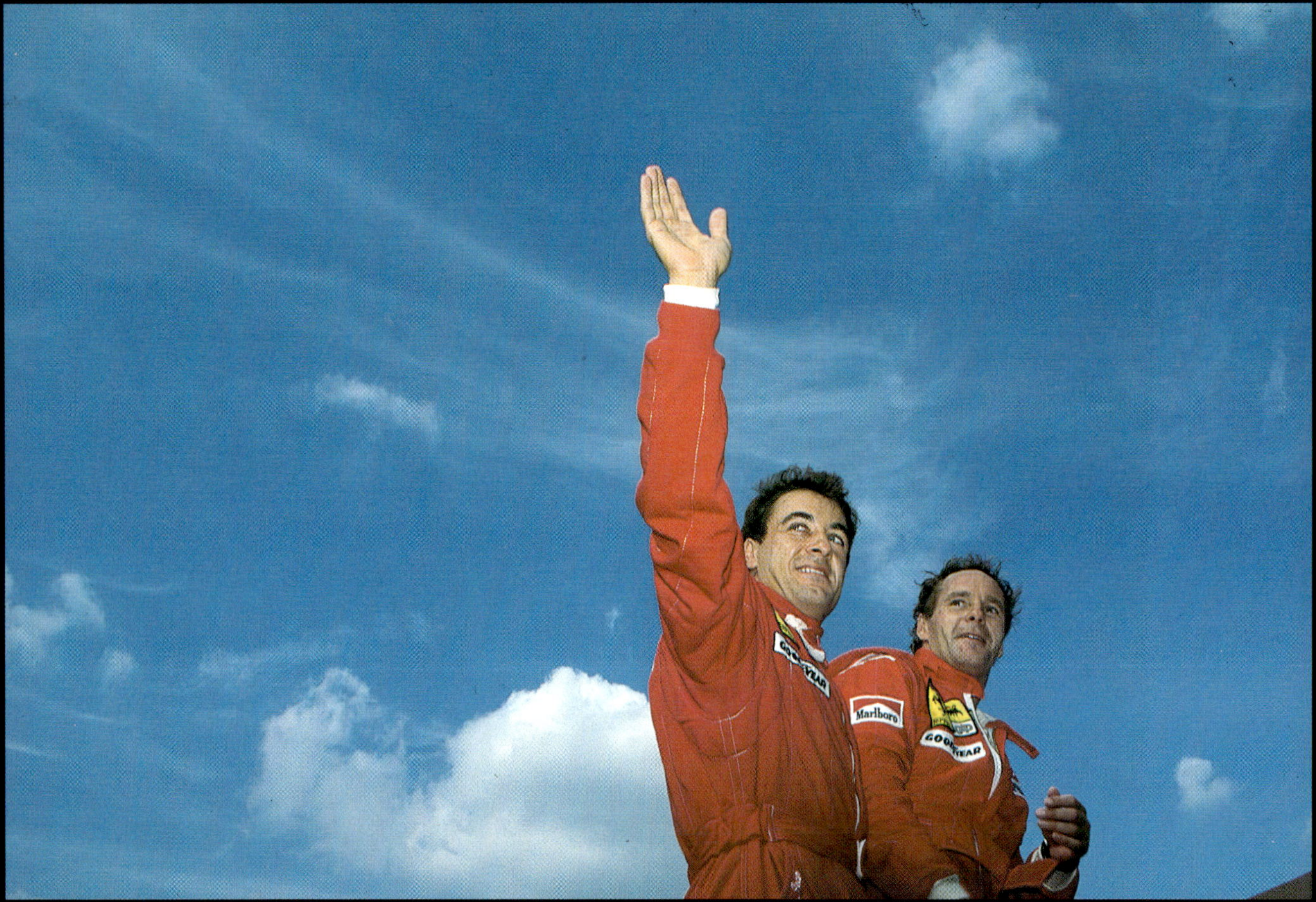

GOODYEAR
Marlboro
GOODYEAR

J. ALESI
Agip
GOODYEAR
Marlboro

MARELLI
Marlboro
27
MAGNETI MARELLI
FIAT
GOODYEAR
Agip

MAGNETI
OMEGA
Marlboro
Marlboro
27
MAGNETI MARELLI
GOODYEAR

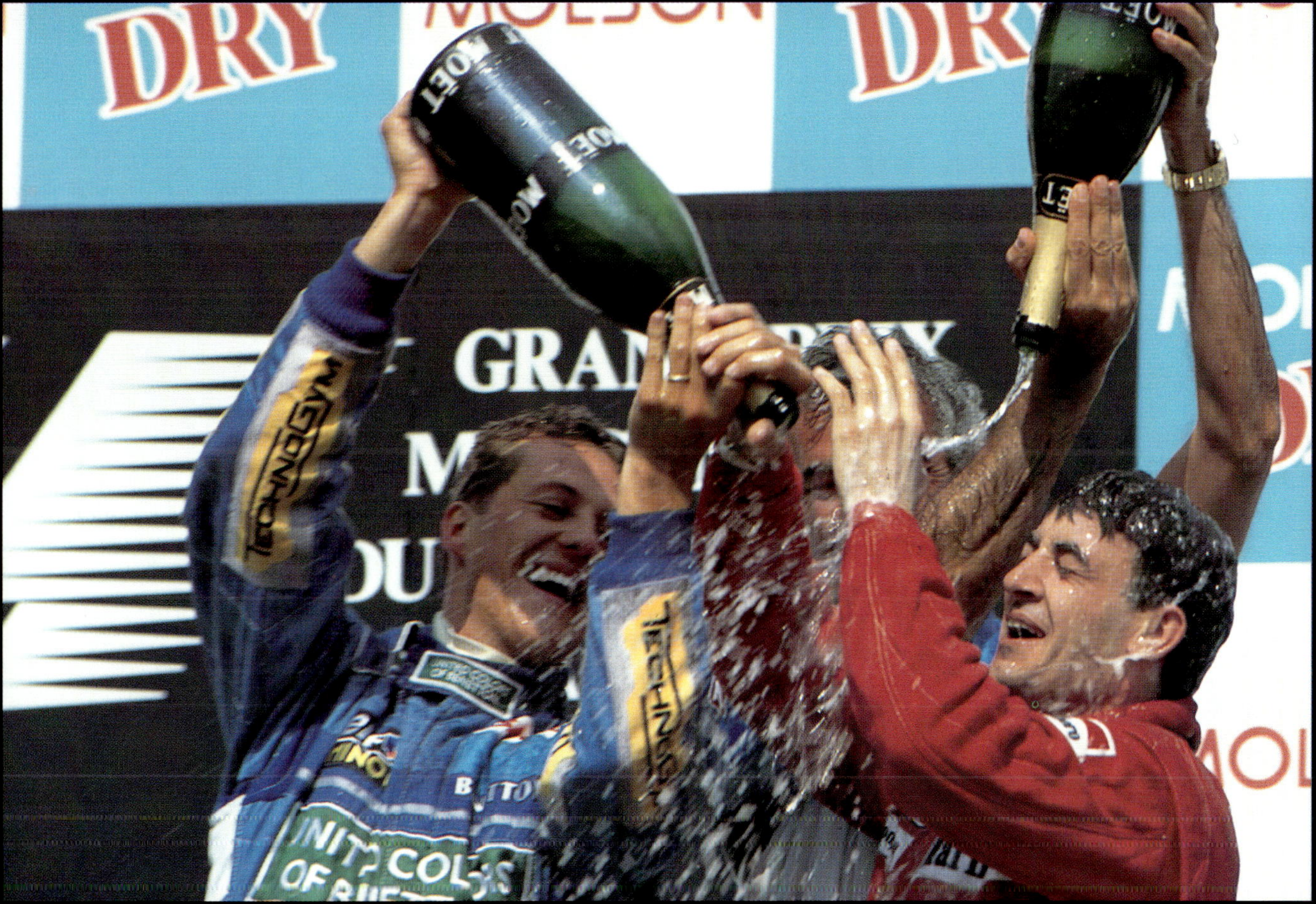
DRY
MOLSON
DRY
MOET
TECHNOGYM

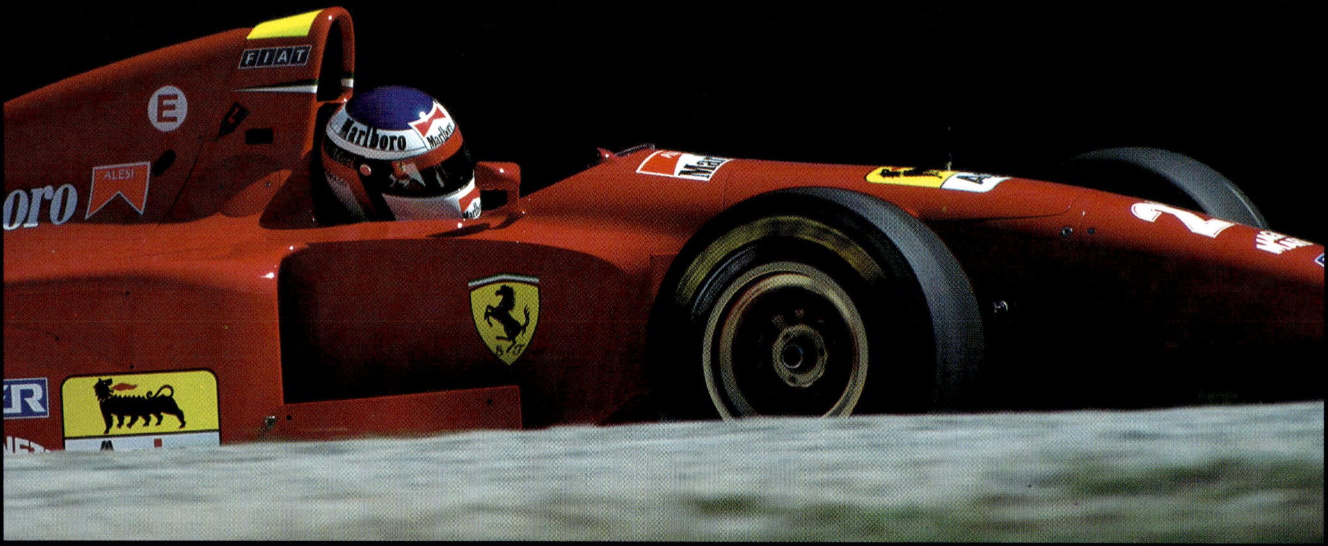
FIAT
ALESI

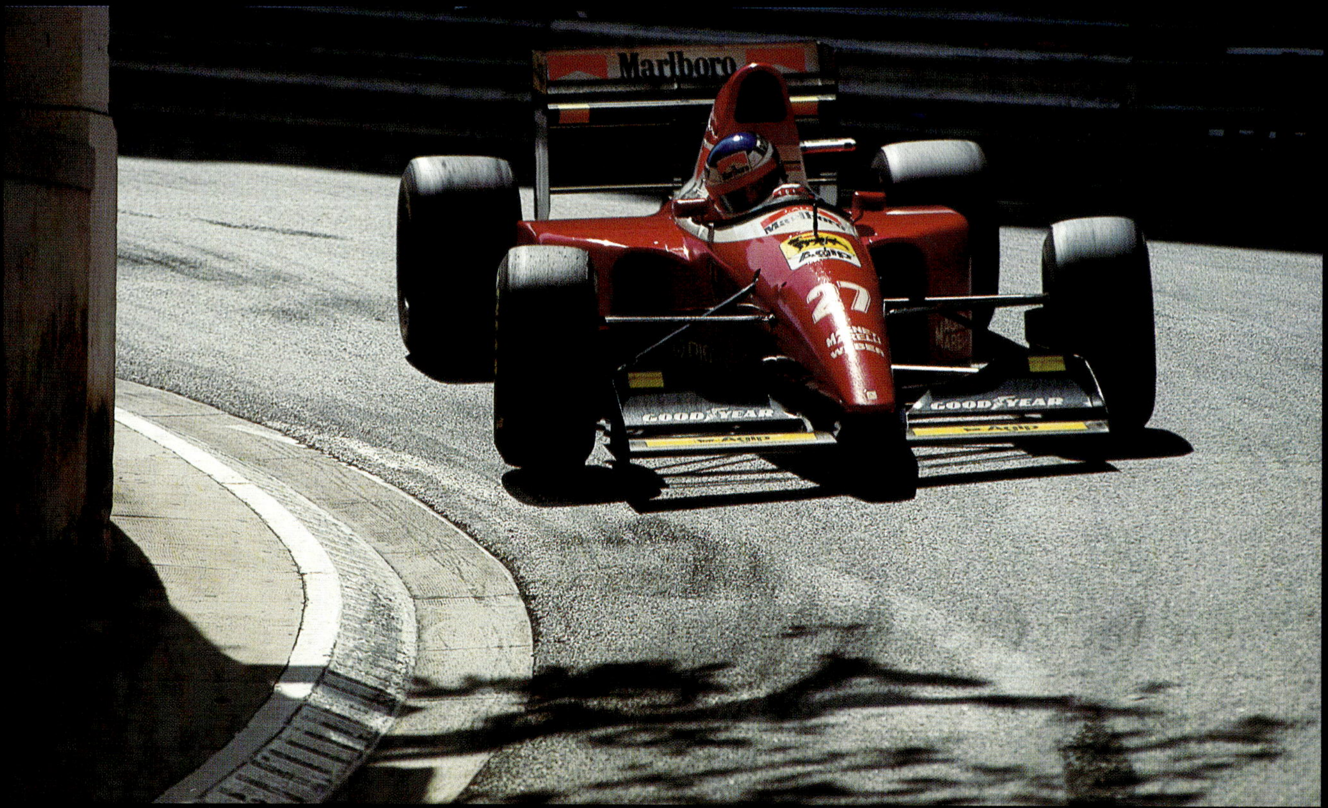
Marlboro
27
GOODYEAR
GOODYEAR

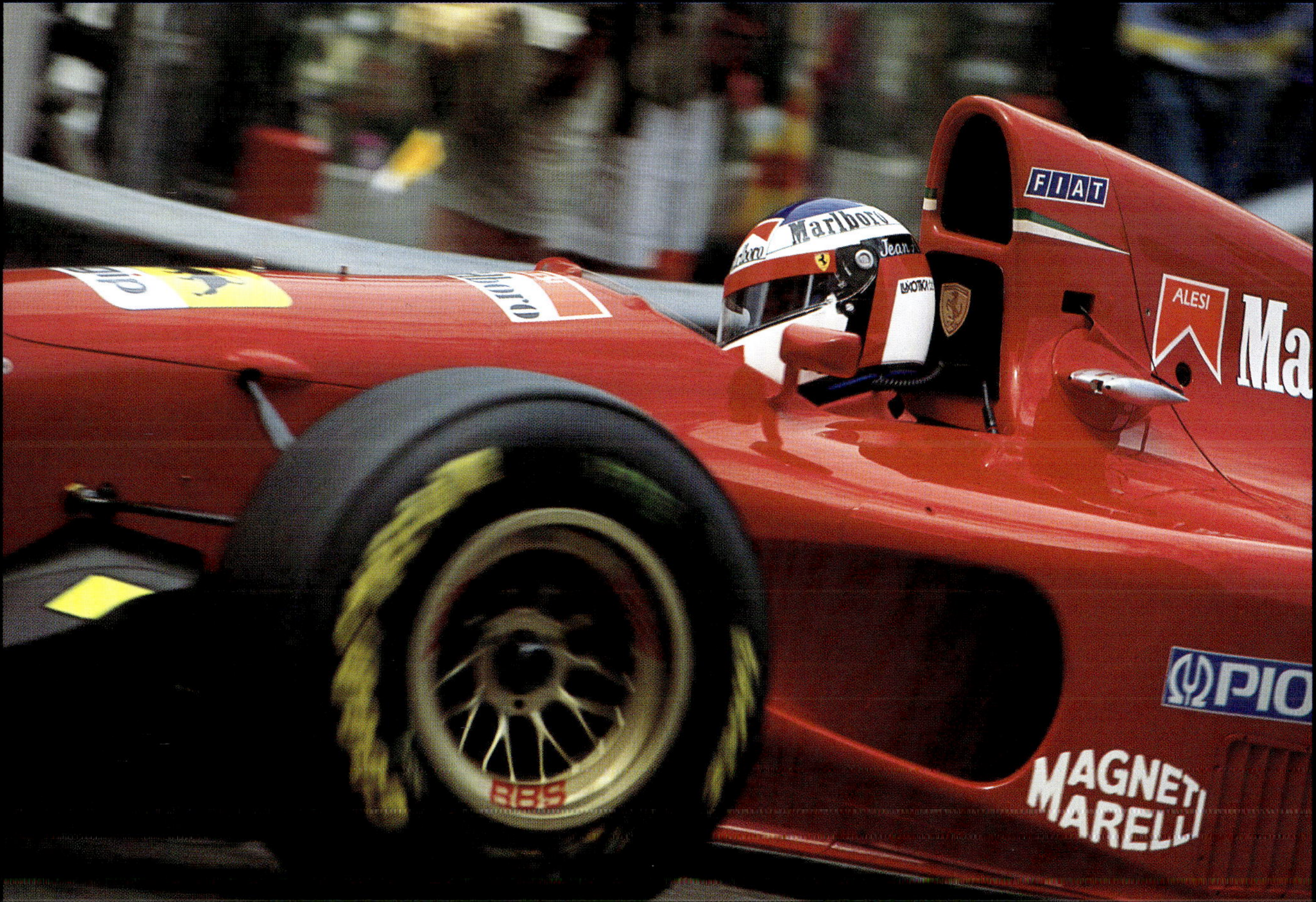
FIAT
ALESI
Marlboro
MAGNETI MARELLI
BBS

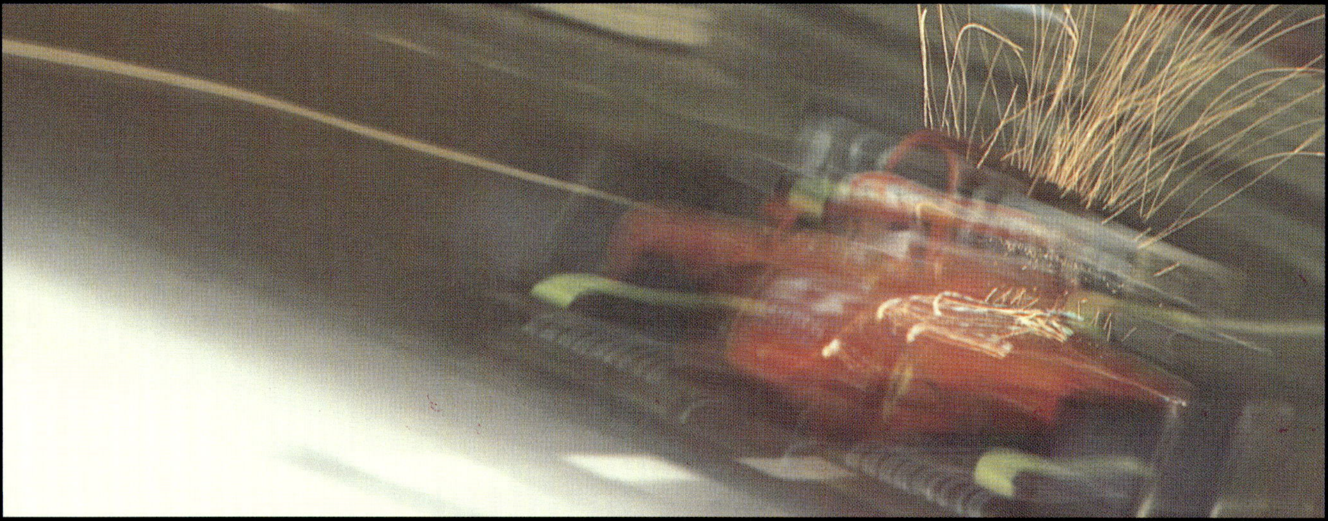

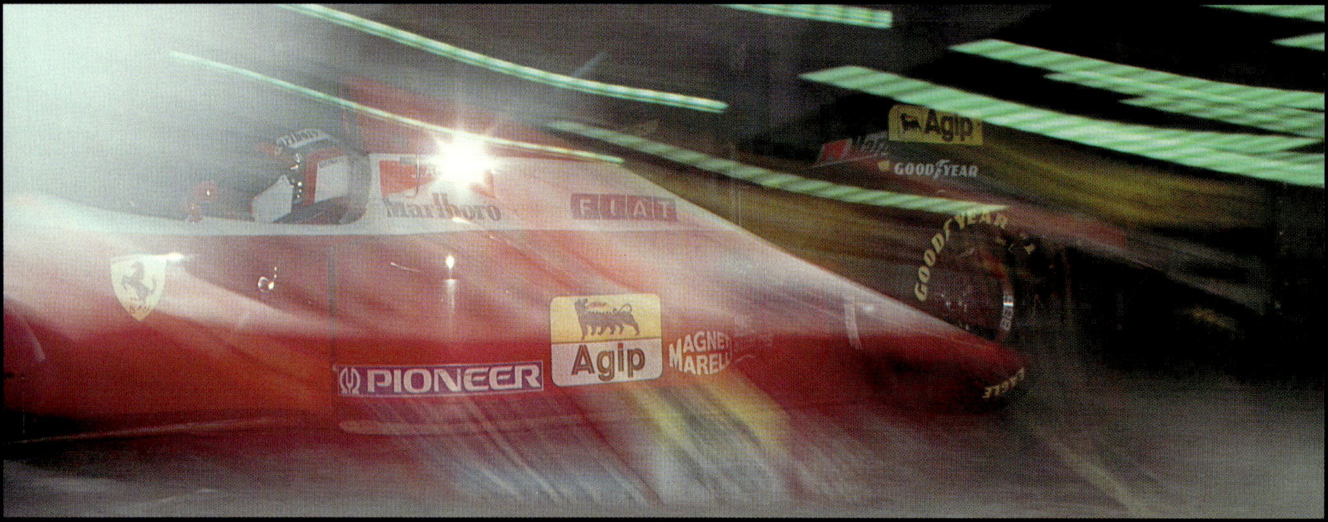
Agip
GOODYEAR
Marlboro
FIAT
Agip
PIONEER

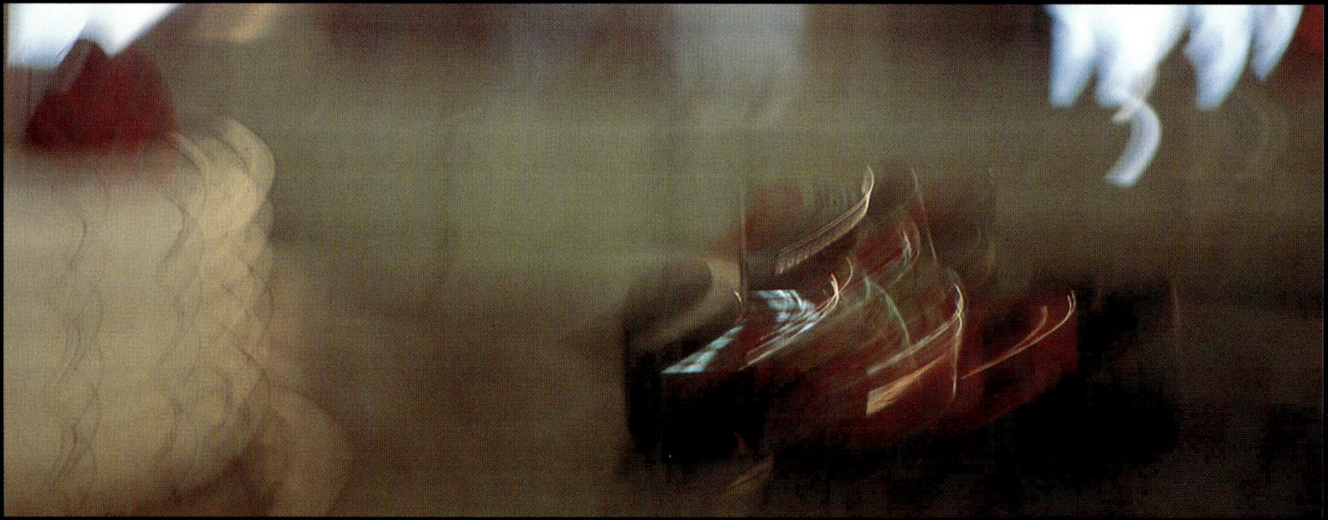

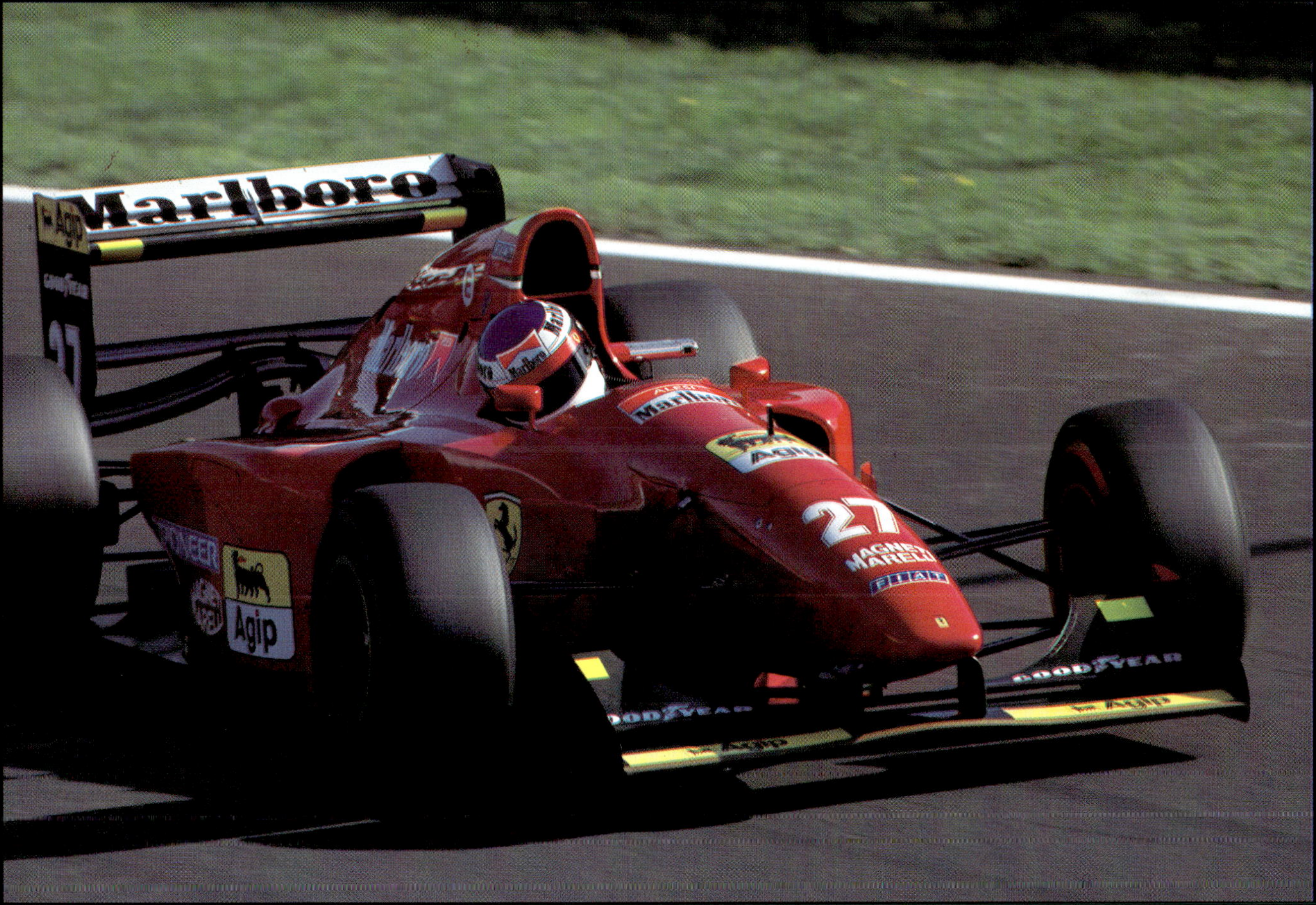
Marlboro
Agip
27
MAGNETI
MARELLI
FIAT
Agip
GOODYEAR

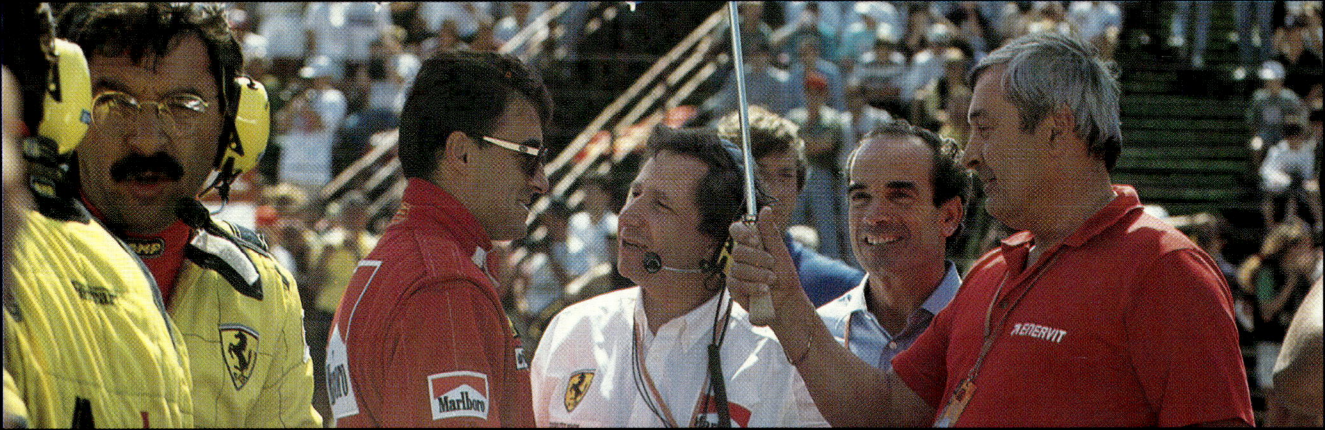
Marlboro
ENERVIT

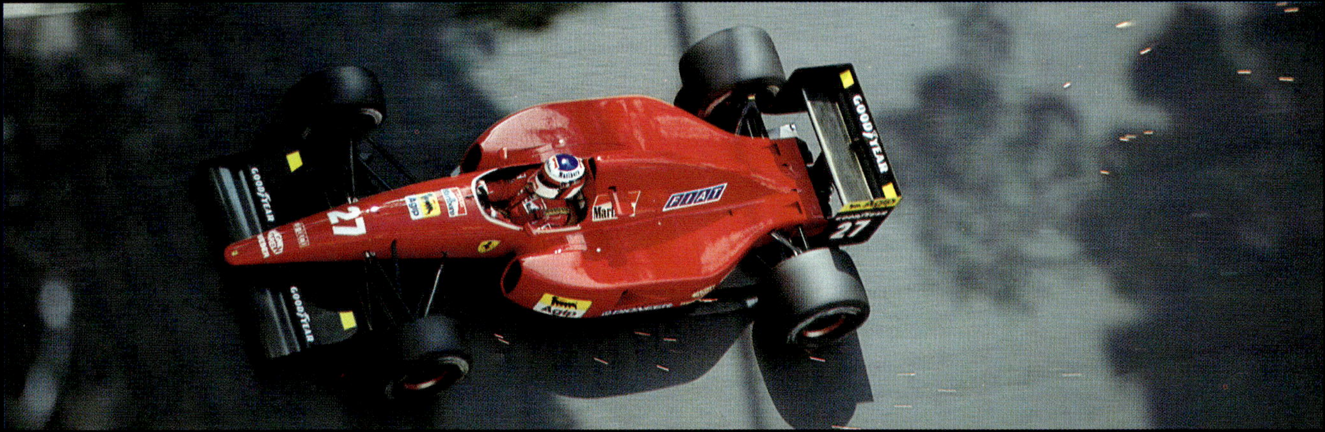
GOODYEAR
FIAT
27
Agip

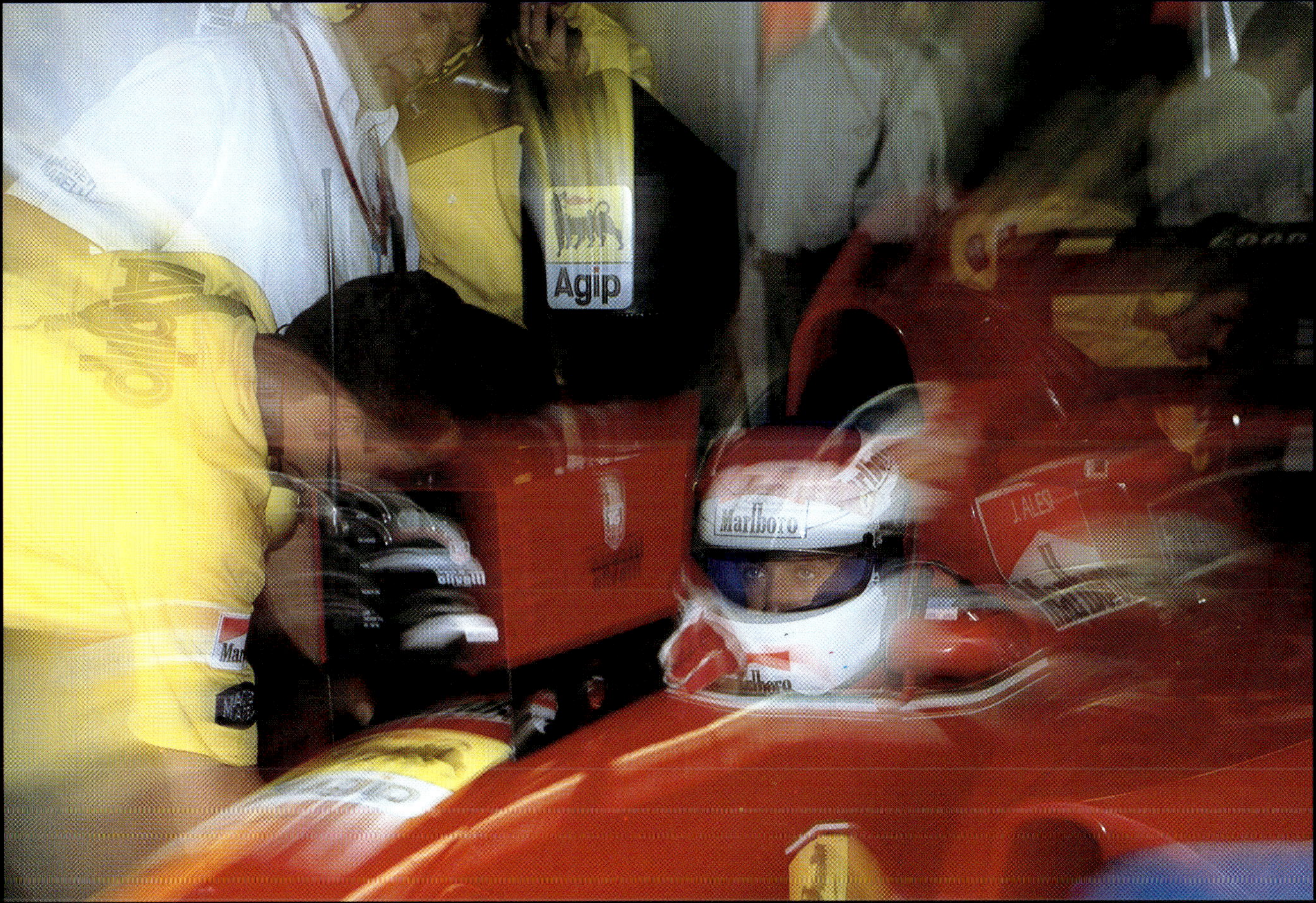
Agip
Marlboro
J. ALESI

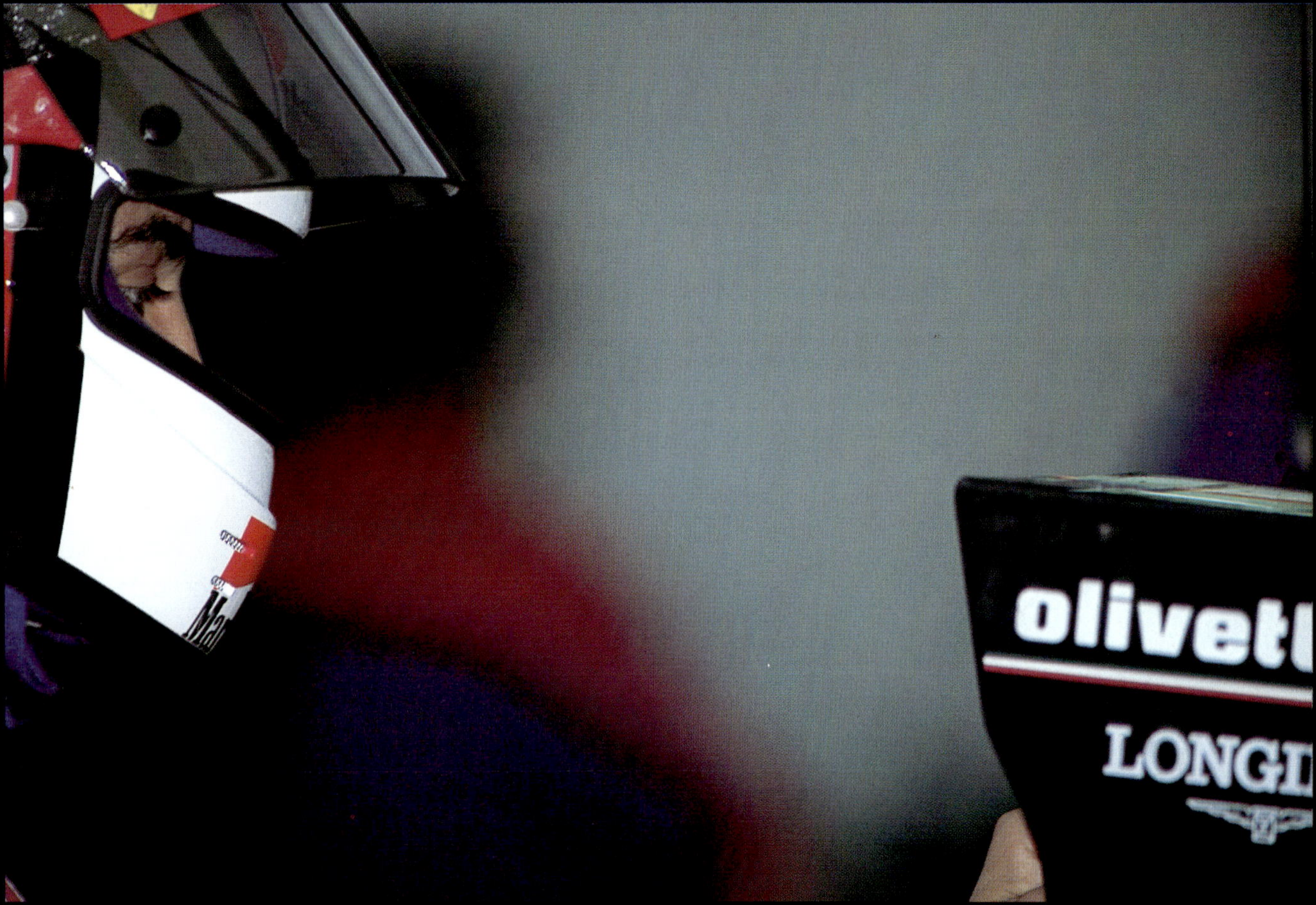
olivett
LONGI

# Chapter 9

# *A Classic Day in Montreal*

The 1995 season showed every sign of impending success for the Scuderia Ferrari. On the basis of the results obtained at the end of the 1994 season, the engineers gathered at the Ferrari GTO branch, based in England and under John Barnard's direction, brought forth the 412T2 chassis. It appeared to be a step in the right direction. Jean Alesi returned from the first test drives filled with enthusiasm, even if the car had been finished at the last moments before the first 1995 Grand Prix event in Brazil.

To everyone's surprise, both drivers were able to finish the Interlagos course. After Michael Schumacher and David Coulthard were disqualified, Gerhard Berger would be named the winner; and Jean came in third place, although he claimed to have suffered during the race, "I'd only driven the 412T2 five or six laps in a row prior to the race; so obviously, seventy-one in a row was a hellish ordeal. Still, it's the best Ferrari I've ever driven.

In Brazil, the Scuderia's cars were left more than one lap behind the leaders in the final. However, in Argentina, for the second event of the season, this isn't the case at all. Jean Alesi takes the lead for a few laps, before he is forced to give it up to Damon Hill. At the finish line, Jean walks away with second place and is overjoyed, "The car is truly wonderful. Today, it was worthy of the Williams...the work we've completed in winter is starting to show results...

At Imola, the third Grand Prix of the season, Jean finishes fifth fastest in the practice runs before coming in second in the final. The victory that he'd awaited so patiently since his arrival in Formula 1 couldn't be far away. "No, it's true. This time, I'm there. I can feel a win is really close. There's not much between us and the best of them," he would spout after the race.

In Spain, he was all set to finish second again when his motor let him down with no warning. At the Monaco Grand Prix, two weeks later, the nightmare of seasons past resurfaced. He'd been up to snuff to take the pole-position, as he'd had the best times from the first practice session, before he's condemned to mope about the pits during the entire second qualifying series: his car had broken down in the morning, and had been pushed to the pits by the race commissioners, which effectively eliminated him from the day's practice runs. While Jean was side-lined, his rivals raced without pity to beat his times, and

105

he kept only fifth position on the grill. A catastrophe reminiscent of the days of yore. In the final, he is hit by Martin Brundle and violently finishes up on the rail.

It's in Canada the glory comes calling on Jean. For his 91st Grand Prix, the man from Avignon will finally bring home his first Formula 1 victory. What's more, the win coincides with his 31st birthday; and to compliment this, he wins in a Ferrari numbered 27, the same number as a local driving hero, Gilles Villeneuve. Before a crowd that had never previously given him a second thought, he brought Ferrari back up into the ranks of the champion auto makers.

Of course, this success had only been possible in thanks to Michael Schumacher's problems, who had a comfortable lead 12 laps from the finish line. But Schumacher would have been out of line in making a row over Alesi's victory: Jean had experienced such bad luck, for so long, that this twist in fate could only be justice. He'd already finished in second place six times in his Formula 1 career, "Honestly, there were times when I'd asked myself what I'd done in my life to deserve such bad luck. When I saw Schumacher on the giant screen, in the pits, lifting his steering wheel, I was going around a hairpin turn at the other end of the circuit. I said to myself that perhaps today was the day. My crew verified what I'd seen on the screen over the radio. I started to cry. This was a problem, because when I braked, the tears would splash against the interior of my visor, and I couldn't see the break walls. So I told myself that it wasn't over 'till it's over, and I had to concentrate until the end. I got a hold of myself, and voila.

Once the checkered flag had been waved, Jean started out on his congratulatory tour. He'd risen up in the car to salute the crowd, and when he sat back down, he stalled out – the car had broken down. Schumacher went and picked up the broken-down hitch-hiker, bringing him to the podium. It was an emotional award ceremony, "It was really moving, because when you drive for Ferrari, you do it for Ferrari's place in automotive history. There's always someone telling you that 19 years ago, on this track, or with that model, or such-and-such place on the grill, someone else who was the same age had won, so you should win, too. So today I'm really happy. All in all, I'd prefer to have my first win in Montreal, at Gilles Villeneuve's home track, with his number, 27. This morning, I'd asked Prost how many times he'd won here. He said once. I told him, "you disappoint me," because, usually, when I ask him this question, he always says three or four times. I told him that if I won, I'd be tied with him. So there you go, I'm up with Prost.

It was Jean's deliverance and it would be vigorously celebrated, "I can assure you it will be a wild night, and it will last all week." It would be a party in proportion with the long wait that had preceded this win, and would continue Tuesday night in Avignon, at the little bar where Jean had hung out with his friends.

The rest of the 1995 season was much more difficult. Jean's performances were a definitive regression from the season before. In Germany, at Hockenheim, where Ferrari had monopolized the first line in 1994, it had to settle for supporting roles in 1995. At the Silverstone, for the English Grand Prix, Jean took second place, due only to the fact that Michael Schumacher and Damon Hill collided, eliminating both of them from the race.

The Scuderia was back in shape by the end of the season. At Monza, a Ferrari should have won. Jean had the lead eight laps from the finish, but abandoned when rear bearing cracked – a break-down too unusual to believe.

At the European Grand Prix, finally, Jean would complete a demonstration of his extraordinary brilliance behind the wheel by choosing to start on slick tires, even though the track was still soft. He keeps the lead for the large part of the race, before he was forced to give it up to Michael Schumacher two laps before the checkered flag.

The end of the 1995 season marks Jean's five-year anniversary with Ferrari. This is one of Ferrari's most enduring relationship with a driver. "At the beginning, it was scary, Ferrari being such a megalith in the history of car racing," Jean recalls today. "Then, you get used to it, and later, you realize what an advantage to work with a crew like we have at Ferrari. There's also the public support, which is really wonderful. No matter where we are, in France, Canada, or Australia, there is always Ferrari fans, with their flags, cheering us on. Sure everything at Ferrari is always changing, sometimes really fast, and that can take a toll on your nerves. Because when things go badly, there's always got to be somebody to blame. Somebody always has to be found guilty, and the person blamed isn't always the one responsible. Luckily, no one ever directly blamed me, even if Luca Di Montezemolo has balled me out more than once for saying more than he wanted said to the press."

Staying with the same team a long time also helps one know the people you work with to a ceratin degree. "Obviously, as time passed, I felt more and more comfortable at Ferrari. By staying five years, you end up knowing how people will react. At the personal level, it's the same thing. I know people better than I did before. People's reactions don't surprise me anymore...Of course, you get into bad habits by staying so long with the same team, but not too many, because everything is so controlled, that it's hard to make too many mistakes.

Jean loved the support of the tifosi and his fans. Also, he complains about the intolerable presence of the paparazzi, the Italian photographers that go to any length to track their victims. "Frankly, it's really hard to take," Jean says, "and the problem is that you have to catch them in the act, or they act all innocent. During my vacation in Capri, right before the Belgian Grand Prix, I caught one. He'd followed me for 20 minutes through the city streets, when I spun around and said, 'Okay, one photo, then I don't want to see you again, and if I do, I'll knock you for one.' And he left. Really, these people have a disgusting occupation. Otherwise, the press doesn't bother me at all. Everyone always says that the Italian press is terrible, that they put a lot of pressure on us. And it's true, they know about everything, all the problems, but from my point of view, I take it as a medium for motivation, without worrying about it too much.

Over the years, Jean has acquired the reputation of "Mister 110%," he who gives all he's got, all the time, whatever the circumstances. However, even if he says he always gives his best, he admits that the car's performance at the technical level greatly influences his driving, "The fact that you have an excellent car at your disposal makes you want to win that much more. We're always working to correct the car's deficiencies in making adjustments. And since I've very rarely had a good car, I give the impression of having a brutal driving style. But I think that my driving style has changed very little over the years I've been with Ferrari. On the other hand, I've made a lot of progress in the manner in which I approach making adjustments.

At the end of 1995, Jean still hadn't employed hindsight regarding his years at Ferrari. But after all the years he'd passed with the Scuderia, he is capable of analyzing the inadequacies of the establishment, "What's particular with Ferrari is it's history. That's the difference between it and all other teams. You can feel the tradition at all the tracks. An entire country is behind the Scuderia. The enthusiasm when we win is enormous; it's unique. But there are problems. I get along quite well with President Montezemolo, who's a great man. But he doesn't come to all the races, and because of this, he often doesn't understand the things that I'd like him to understand. Jean Todt restructured the pit crew well, but it's still weighty and complicated. In my opinion, 1996 will be a crucial year for Ferrari. If we fail, heads will roll.

We've seen him before very tense, but from now on, Jean in a man at peace. After winning the Canadian Grand Prix, he admits himself to feel more at ease, as if a huge weight had been lifted from his shoulders. Jean's new life starts next January 1.

# Chapter 10 — *Geneva, a Peaceful Pitstop*

Jean spends his free time between Avignon, where his parents still live, and Geneva, where he's chosen an abode at number 6 on the Rue des Granges, in the old town.

Jean easily admits that life has been good to him so far. At the end of this year of 1995, he has what many men dream of having: a fiancee who is a top model, a profession he loves, a Ferrari in the garage, an apartment in Switzerland...and a few million dollars in the bank, "But don't believe the hype. Switzerland isn't the fiscal paradise it's made out to be," Jean clarifies, "the Swiss are really strict, highly professional, and play by very clear rules. I'm forced to rent an apartment for an enormous sum, and keep a business operating with employees...but I do pay less taxes than I would in France, it's a fiscal relief. I have to do this now, because a driver like me won't be making these amounts of money forever. I have to protect my capital to a maximum. All sportsmen have to do this." He hasn't yet thought about going back to France, because for now, he's concentrating on his career as a race car driver.

At the advice of friends, Alain Prost among them, Jean decided to move to Switzerland. "I'm really happy about it. Alain lives in a little village, but I prefer Geneva. It's a very international city, and I've developed my little habits, like going to the restaurant Valentino, where I like to eat; I have my favorite shops, etc. For me, Geneva equals relaxation. When I'm here, it's the only time in the year I get to slow down. At all other times, it's races, or private trials...When I'm here, I try to stay for three days in a row, so I can spend one day in Chamonix. Sometimes I go there with Kumiko. We take the lift to the Aiguilles du Midi, walk a ways towards the glacier fields, and come back down on the train. We take off with a backpack, and it's fabulous...

"When I'm in Geneva, I don't even do any physical training, I just rest. In Avignon, it's not okay to invite all my friends over to my parents house. If I go there, it's only to say 'hi' to everyone. In Geneva, I have friends that go as far back as the Formula Renault époque. I could have a lot more friends, the people I call 'my new friends,' if you catch the drift, but I don't like this type of person.

Geneva's tranquillity doesn't mean a total respite from autograph searchers. "People ask me more often in Geneva than in Avignon. It's not unbearable, but people ask for autographs quite often. Each time I go out, I sign three or four. This doesn't bother me at all. One time I was walking along on the sidewalk, and a bus stopped next to me. The driver opened the doors and asked me for an autograph while all his passengers were made to wait. You can say 'no' under circumstances like that...People seem to enjoy making contact with me. When I bought furniture, the salesman closed the store to bring me the furniture himself, etc. It's nice to be recognized, for sure. In any case, I couldn't live in a place that I didn't have any friends...

Jean says he doesn't go out often, and never went to night clubs or discoteques. Anyway, he spends most of his days on the road, "In Geneva, I never take the car out, it's too much of a bore. But I'm never too far from Italy. It takes just a few hours to get to Maranello..." Jean admits to having covered around 50,000 kilometers a year in his Ferrari road car, "Every time I leave it off at the factory for tuning, the guys ask me what I do with it to get it into such a state...well, when I drive, I drive!

# Chapter 11 — *From Red to a Rainbow*

Jean has been much more than just another driver for the Scuderia Ferrari. After driving for more than five years for the team at Maranello, Jean knows everybody here, from the head engineer to the janitor.

Jean practically has Ferrari in his blood. With him, it was the first time for a long time that the Scuderia had a driver for whom Ferrari was a part of his lifestyle and held such a dear place in his heart.

The moment he realized that the Scuderia sought to appropriate Michael Schumacher's services was a painful one for Alesi, "We were not very happy about the manner in which these events came to pass," Jose Alesi explained, "Niki Lauda, Ferrari's counselor, declared that it was absolutely necessary to have Schumacher under contract, because he was always one second a lap faster than everybody else. From the moment he heard about that, Jean Todt (the sports director at Ferrari) completely forgot Jean. He was really hurt, because basically, it's a divorce: okay, they wanted Michael Schumacher and wanted to drop Jean, fine, but they could have done it in a much more decent fashion.

What Jean really didn't appreciate was the way the Scuderia had held secret negotiations with Schumacher, while denying there was any interaction.

In 1996, Jean will thus leave the team in red for a place behind the wheel of the United Colors of Bennetton. He said he had the choice, at the beginning of summer, to go to Williams, but he had opted for the pit crew that had helped Michael Schumacher twice take the world title.

"I'll start a new life with Bennetton," was Jean's comment, when the signing of the contract was officialized, just after the Hungarian Grand Prix 1995. I think 1996 will be a positive experience in every sense. I'll meet some new people; I'll have a new motor and chassis. These people have made the cars for the world champion. It will be a great point of comparison for me. As difficult as it seemed to beat Senna, I think that Schumacher is within my reach. We'll see next year...

A page in history turns for Jean Alesi. After five years that oscillated between a dream and a nightmare at Ferrari, he will begin a new chapter – that will perhaps be the subject of another book, a long way down the road.

# Photo legends

| | |
|---|---|
| Page 113 | The 1995 season started off much better than the years precedent, even if it starts in a car that not yet broken-in. Brazilian Grand Prix, Interlagos, 1995. |
| Page 114 | Kumiko, Jean's new girlfriend. |
| Page 115 | When Jean is with her, he is always in the best of spirits. The starting grill at the French Grand Prix, Magny-Cours, 1995. |
| Page 116 | The podium so long awaited. Canadian Grand Prix, Montreal, 1995. |
| Page 117 | Returning from the press conference, everyone wants to congratulate the hero of the day. Canadian Grand Prix, Montreal, 1995. |
| Page 118-119 | Upon return from his victory in Canada, Jean's friends had organized a little party in the streets of Avignon in honor of their hero. |
| Page 120 | Pensive, Jean Alesi prepares an end to his five years of loyal service for the Scuderia. |
| Page 121 | Exiting a briefing held by the Scuderia in the mobile workshop. Spanish Grand Prix, Barcelona, 1995. |
| Page 122 top | A relaxing stroll through the streets of Geneva between the Italian and Portuguese Grand Prix. All the while signing autographs and taking phone calls. |
| bottom | In front of number 6, rue des Granges, in the heart of Geneva's old town. Jean lives in a spacious five room apartment on the second floor. |
| Page 123 | Jean admits he's no "cordon blue," even if he loves to make the effort. |
| Page 124-127 | In the living room. |

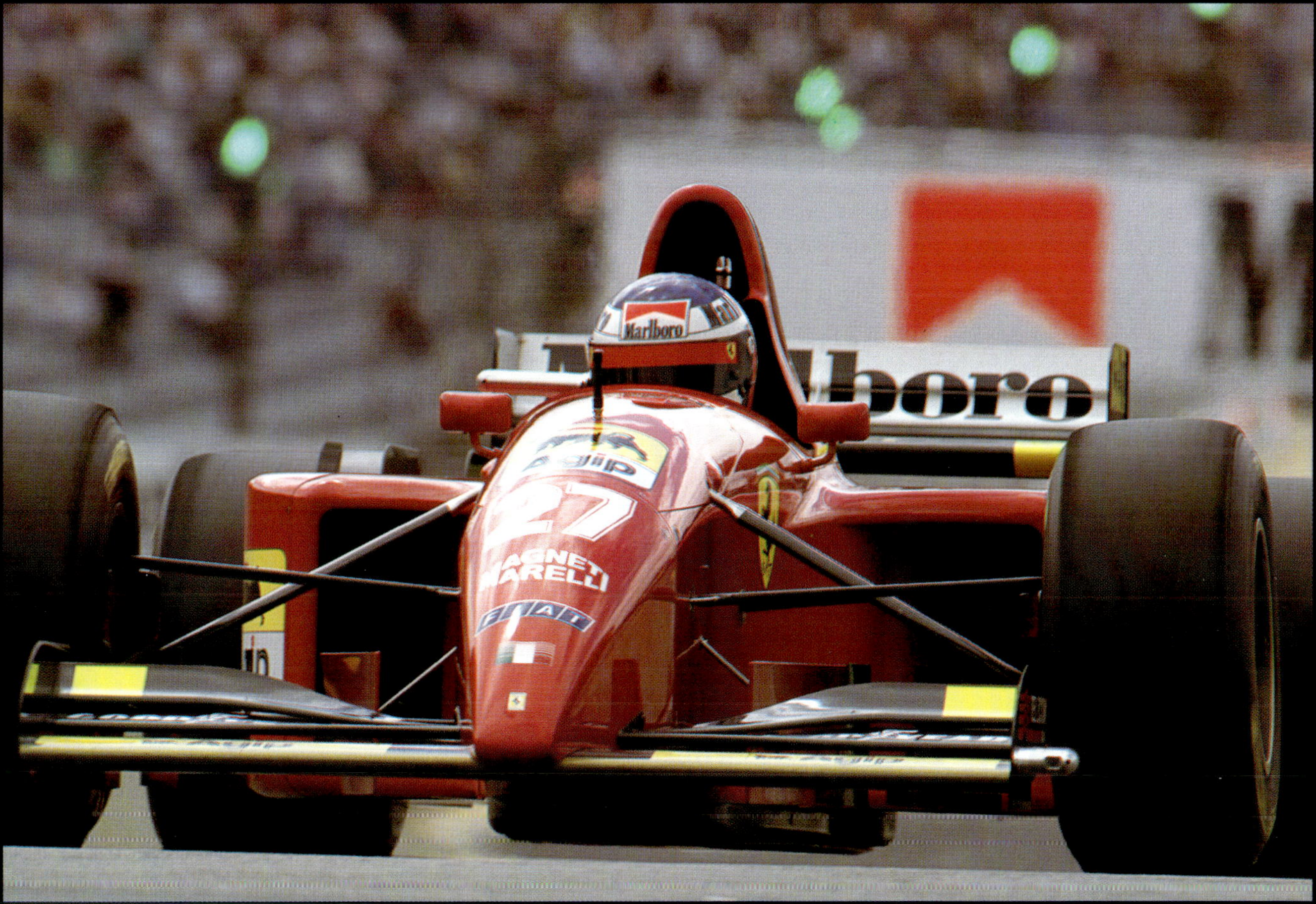
Marlboro
Marlboro
Agip
27
MAGNETI MARELLI
FIAT

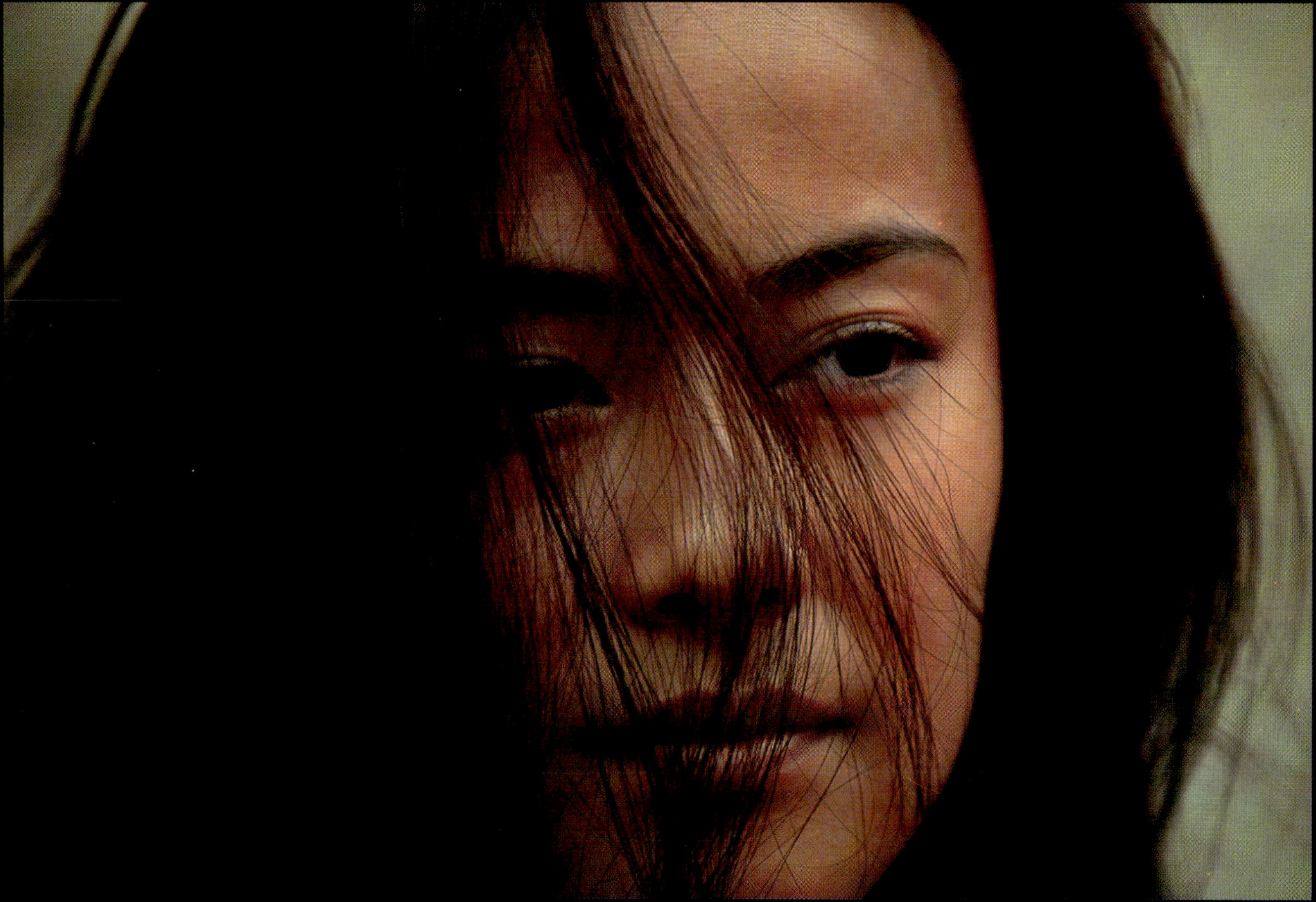

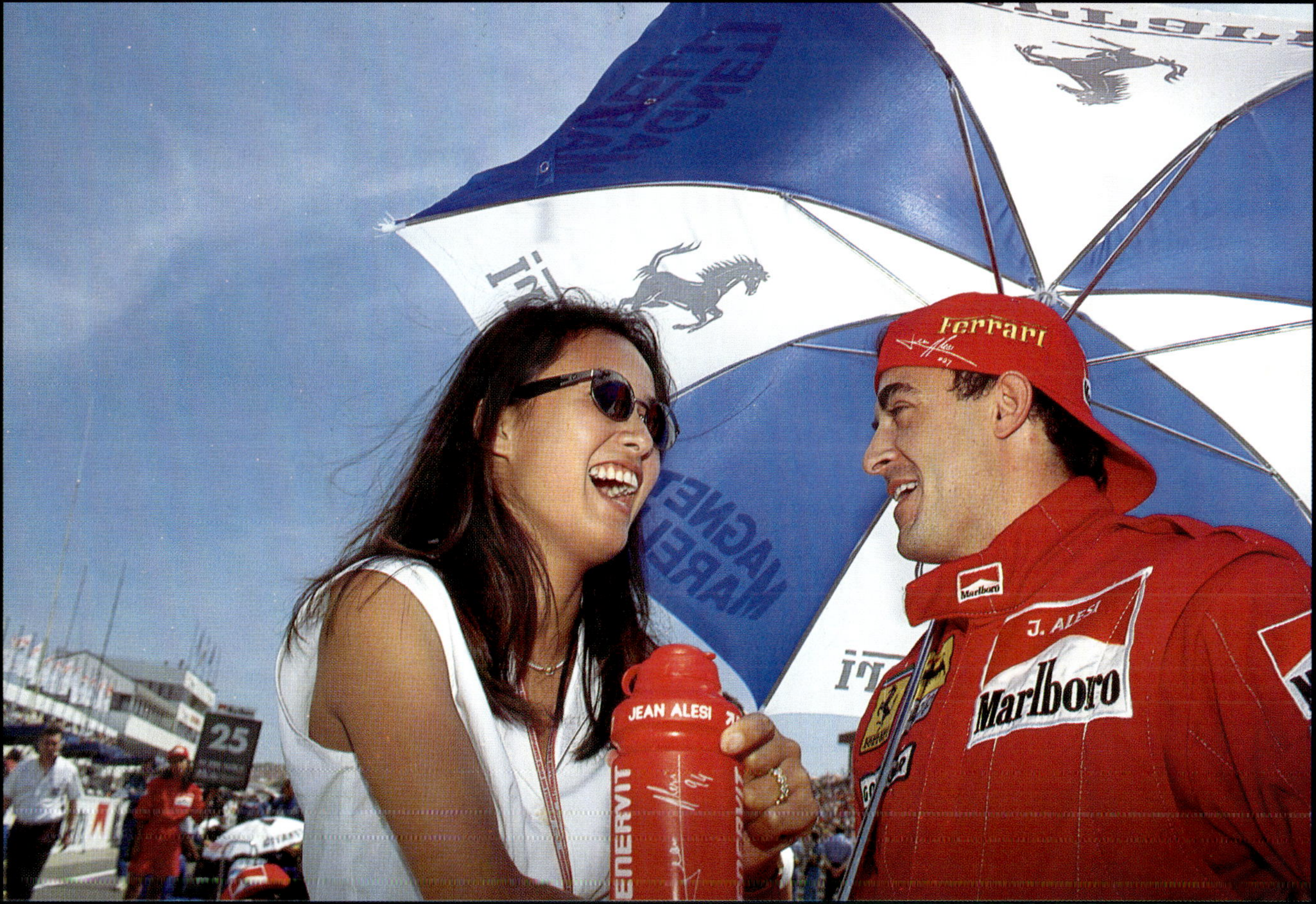
Ferrari
J. ALESI
Marlboro
JEAN ALESI
ENERVIT
25

MOET
GOODYEAR
Marlboro
1995

Ferrari
Agip
GOODYEAR
J. ALESI
Marlboro

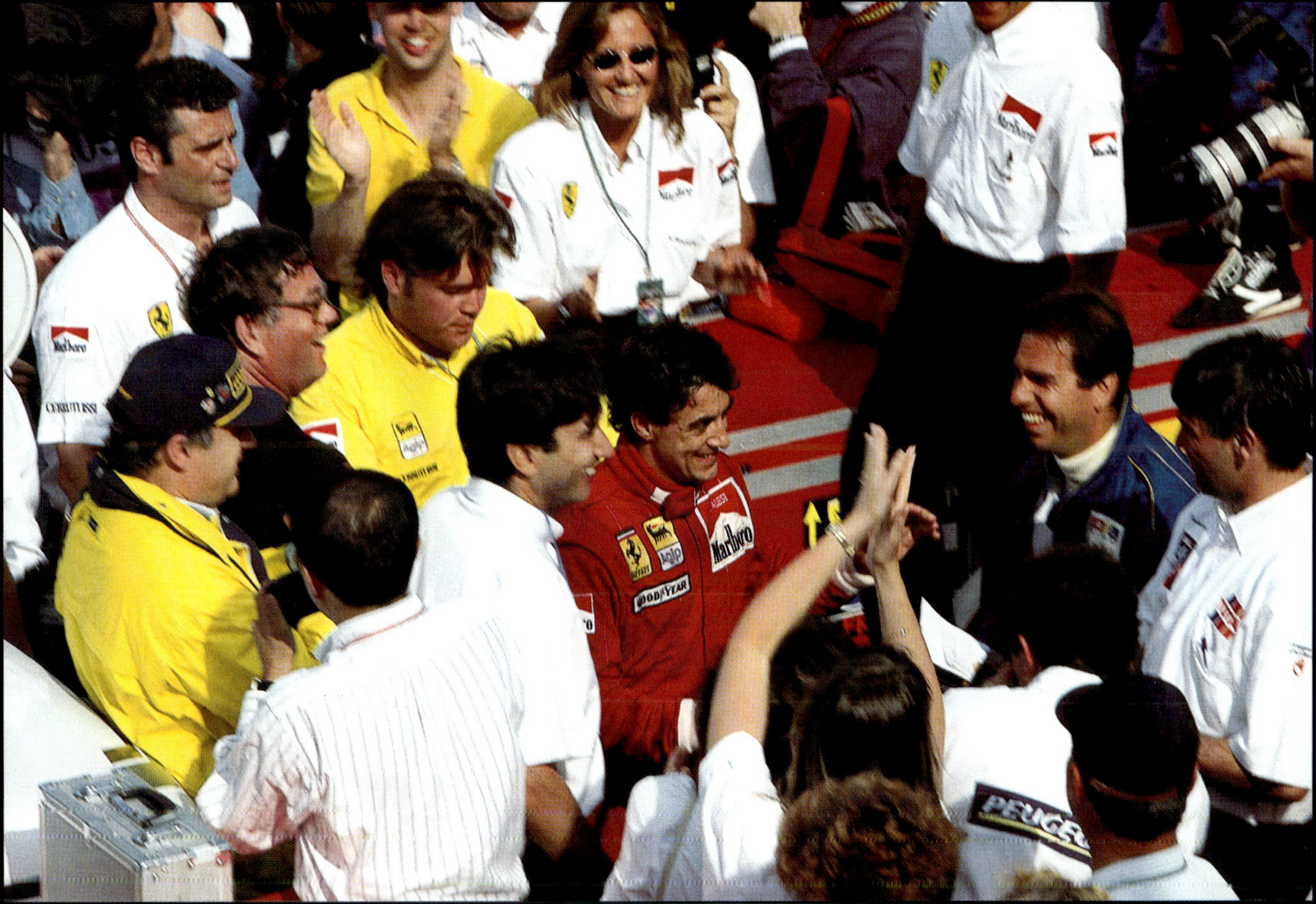

ALESI
Marlboro
GOODYEAR

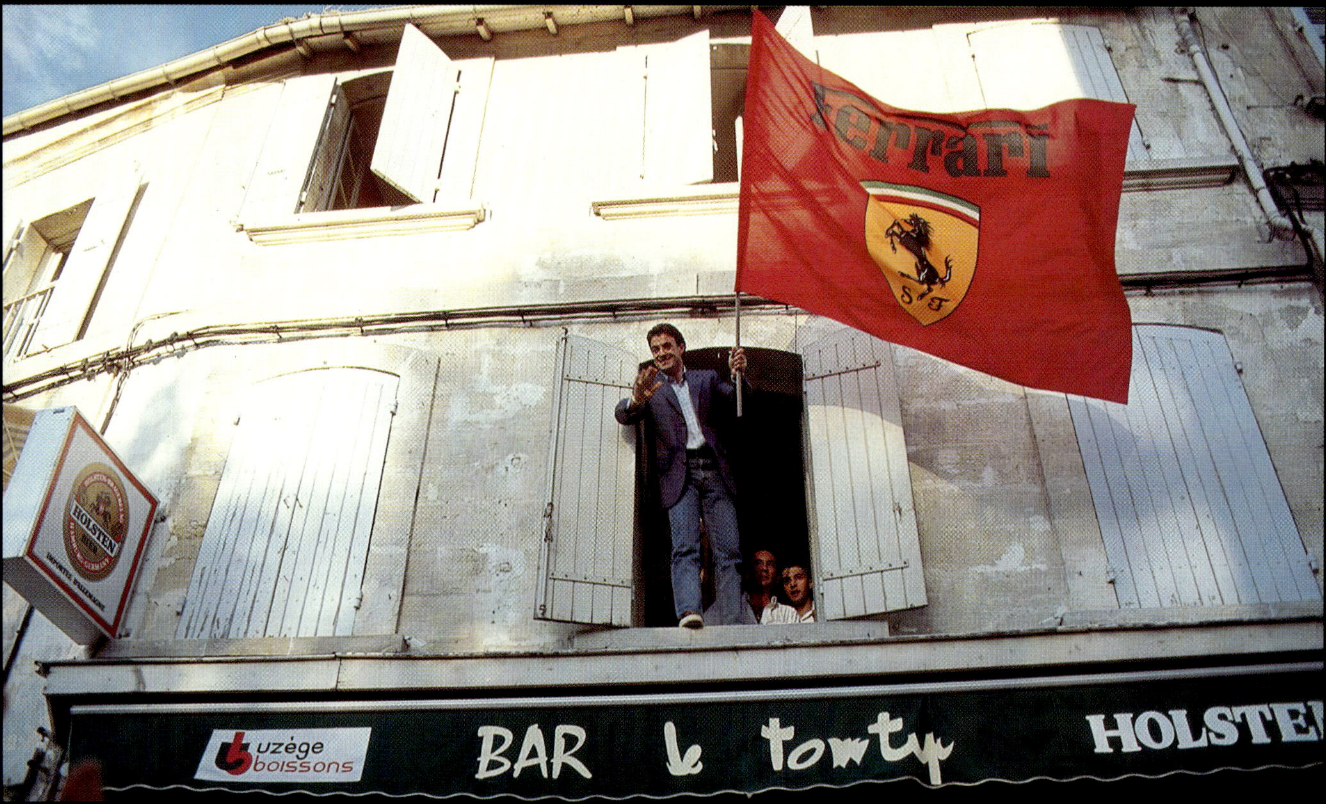
Ferrari
uzège
boissons
BAR

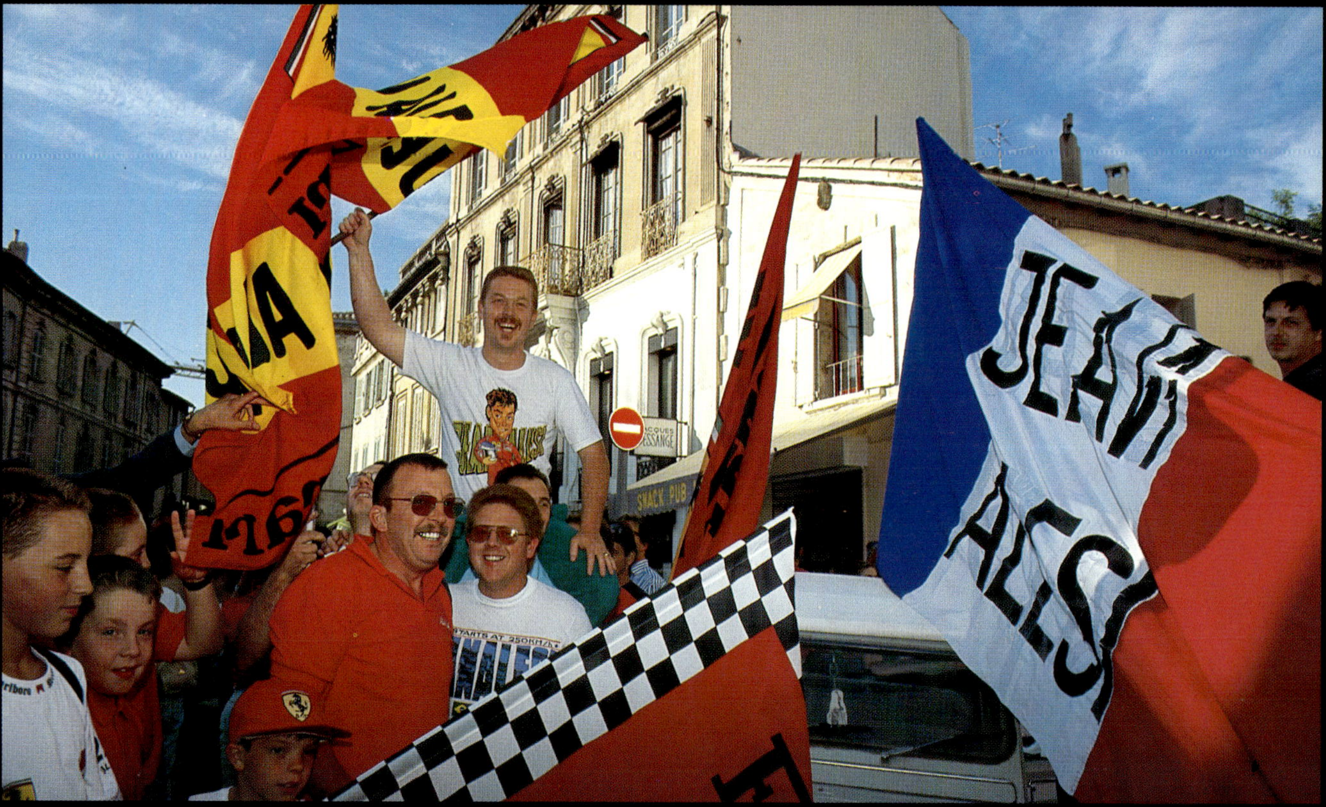
SNACK PUB

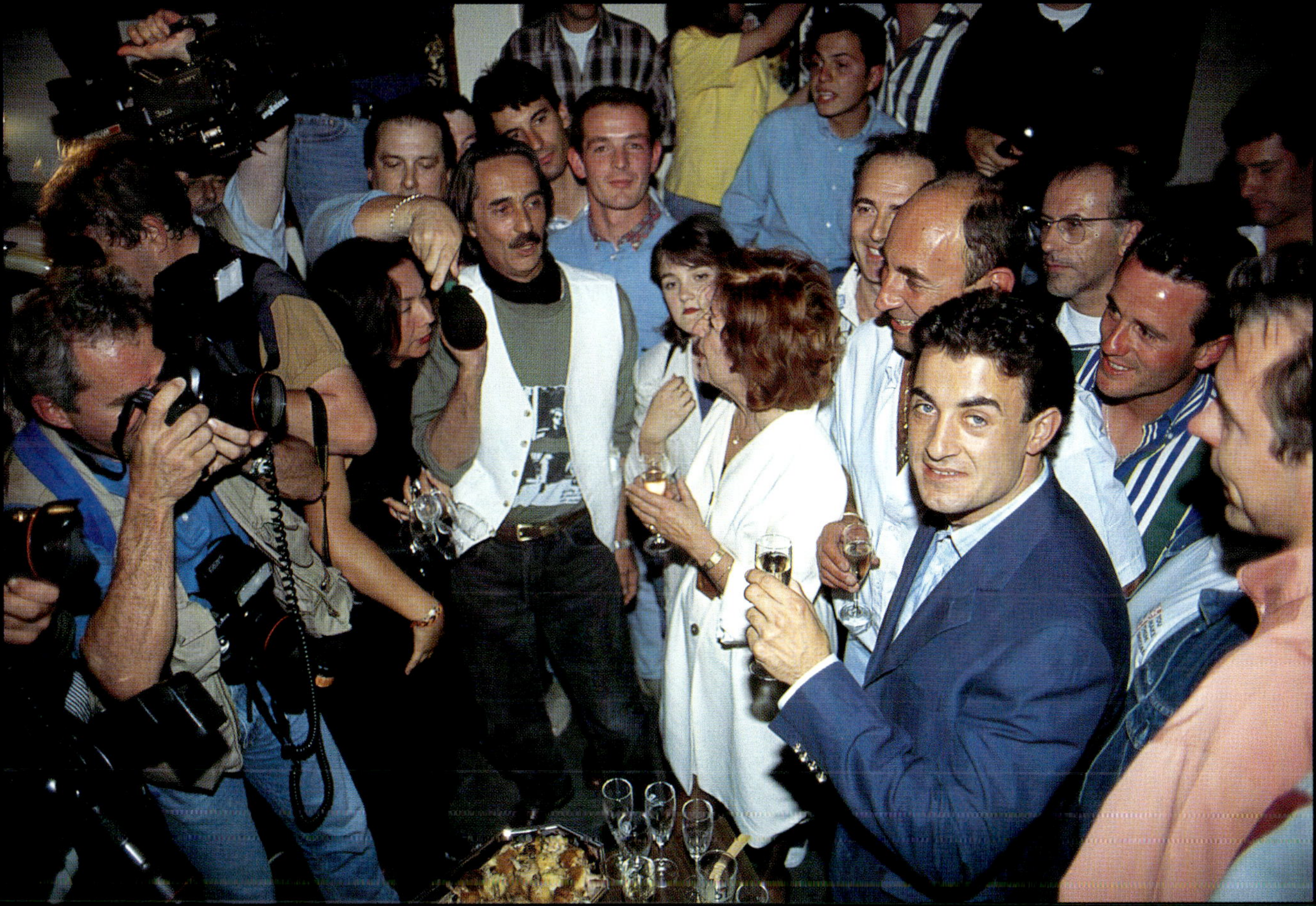

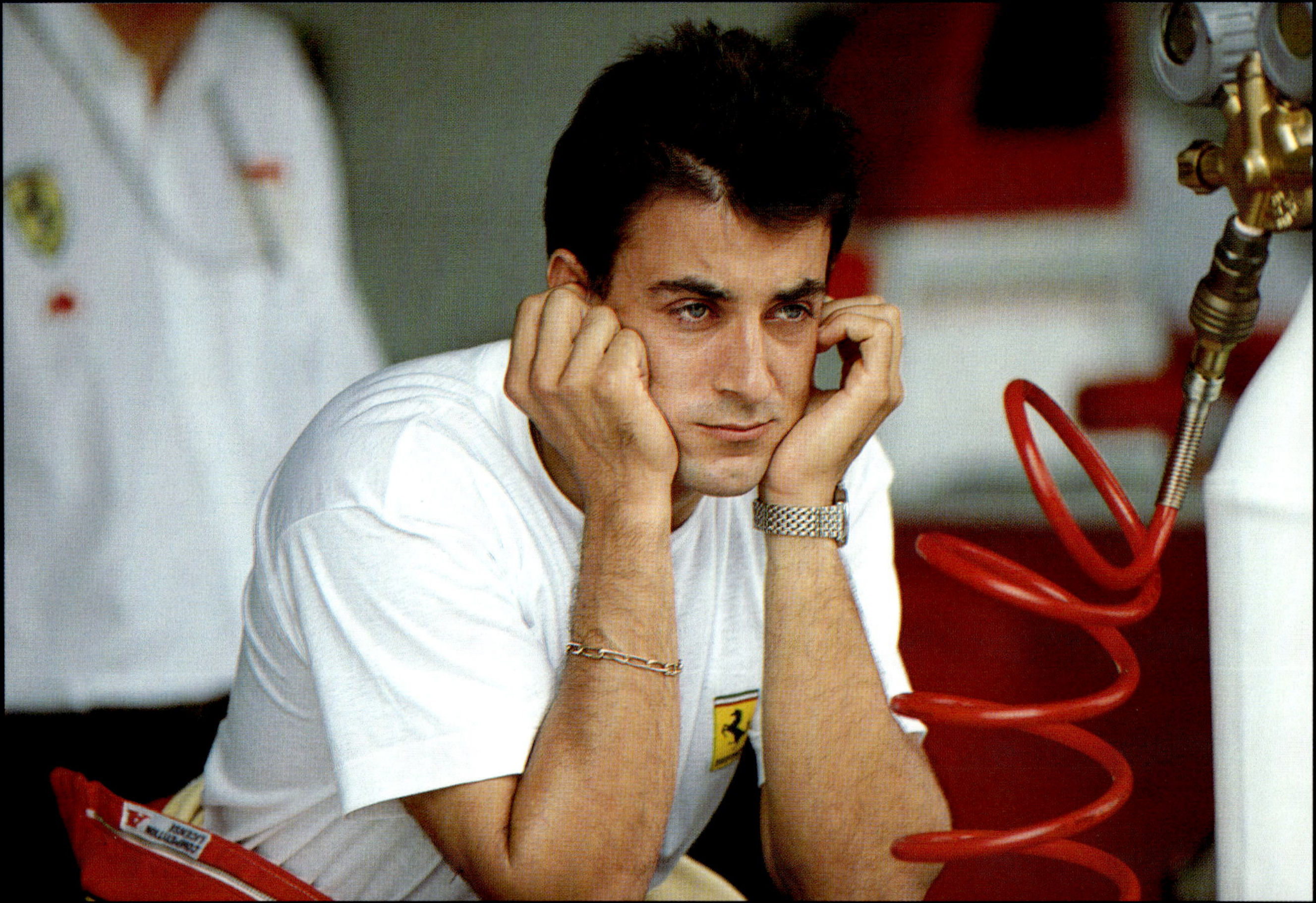

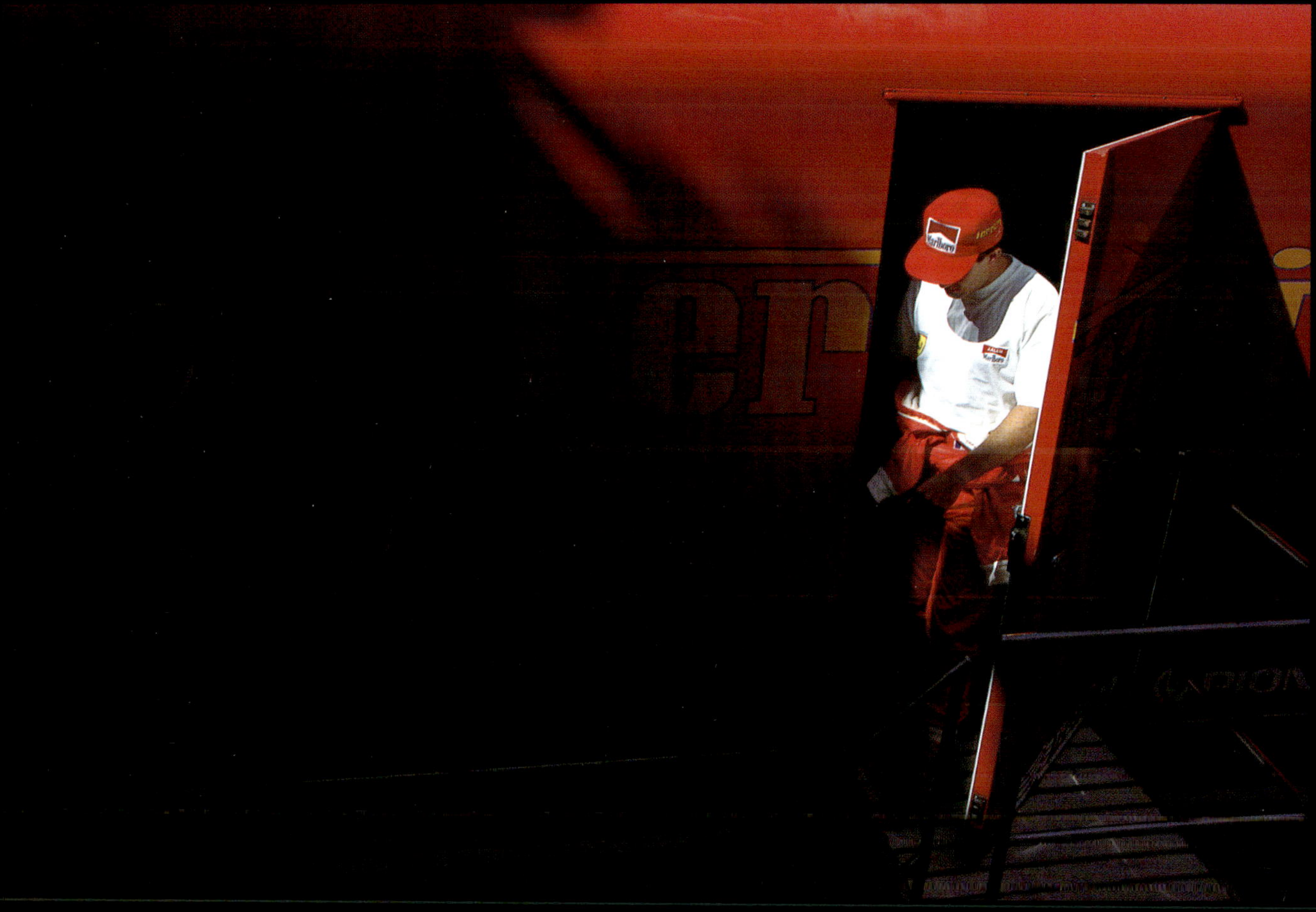
Marlboro

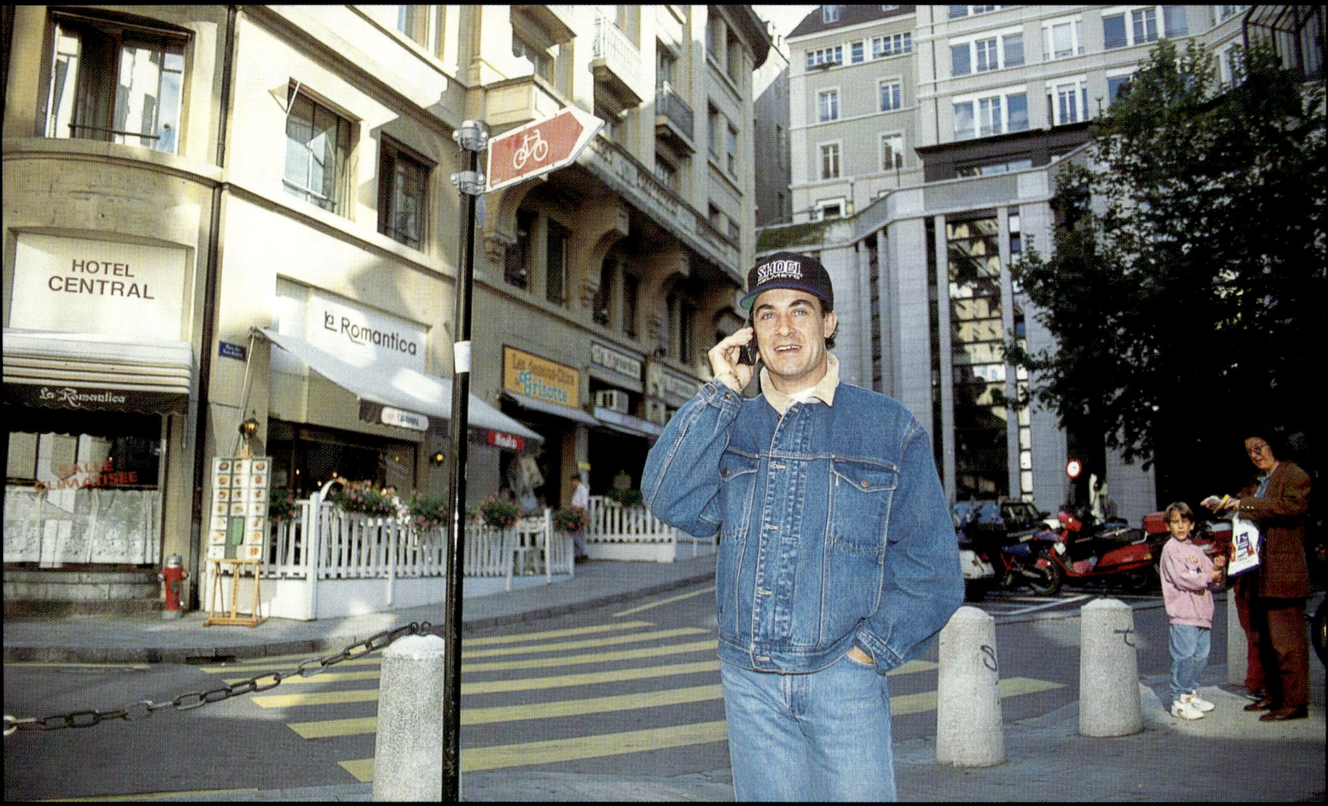
HOTEL
CENTRAL
La Romantica

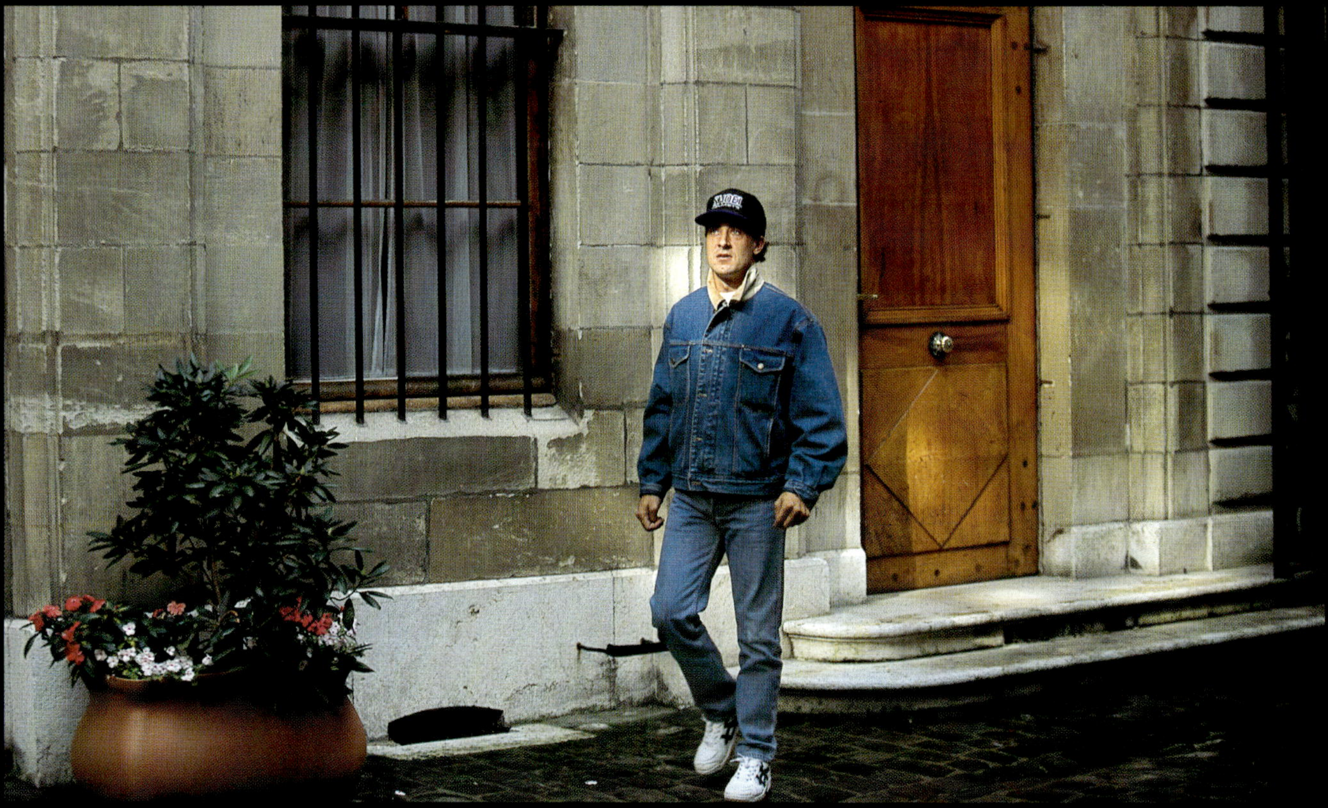

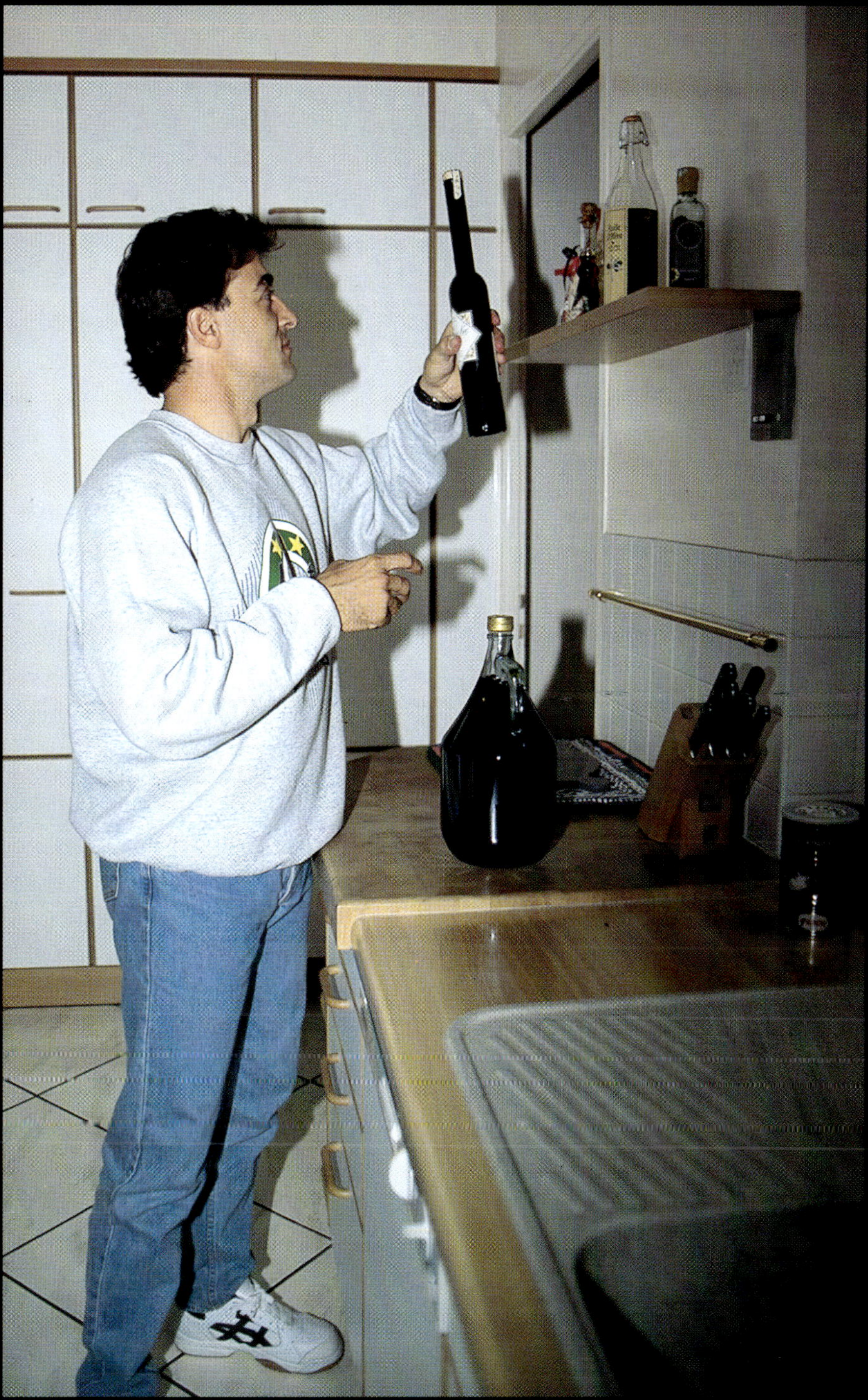

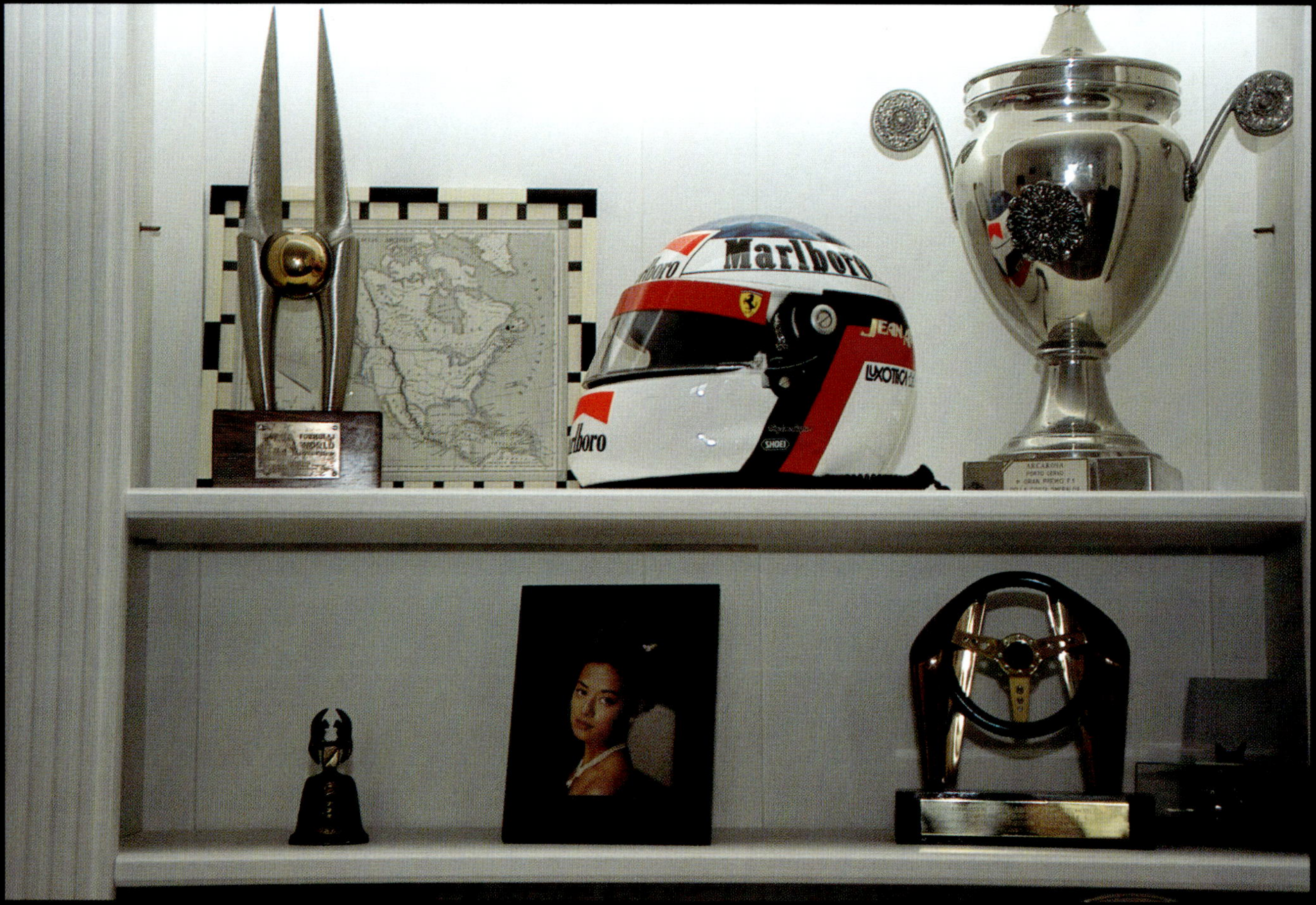
Marlboro
Marlboro
LUXOTTICA
SHOEI

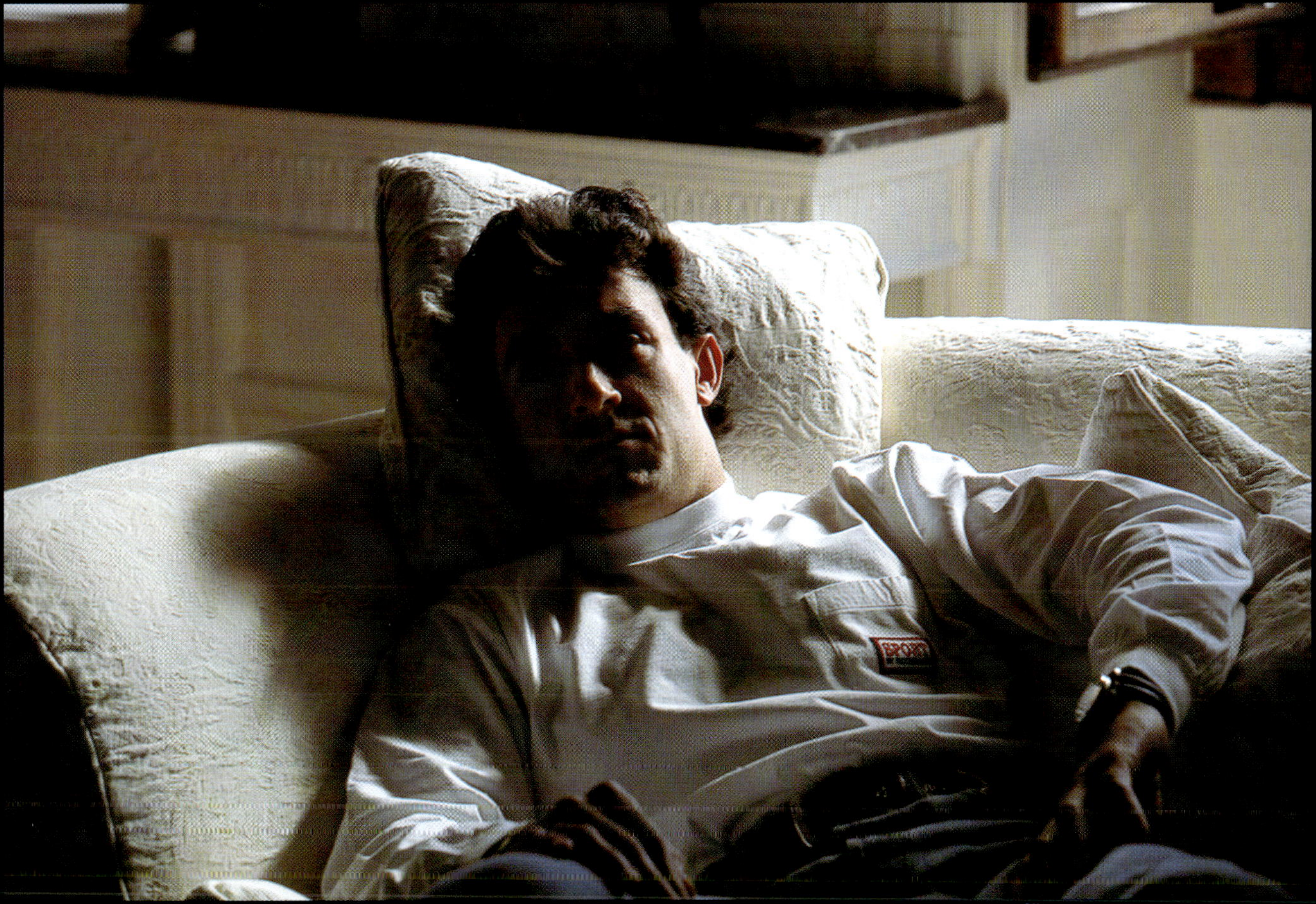

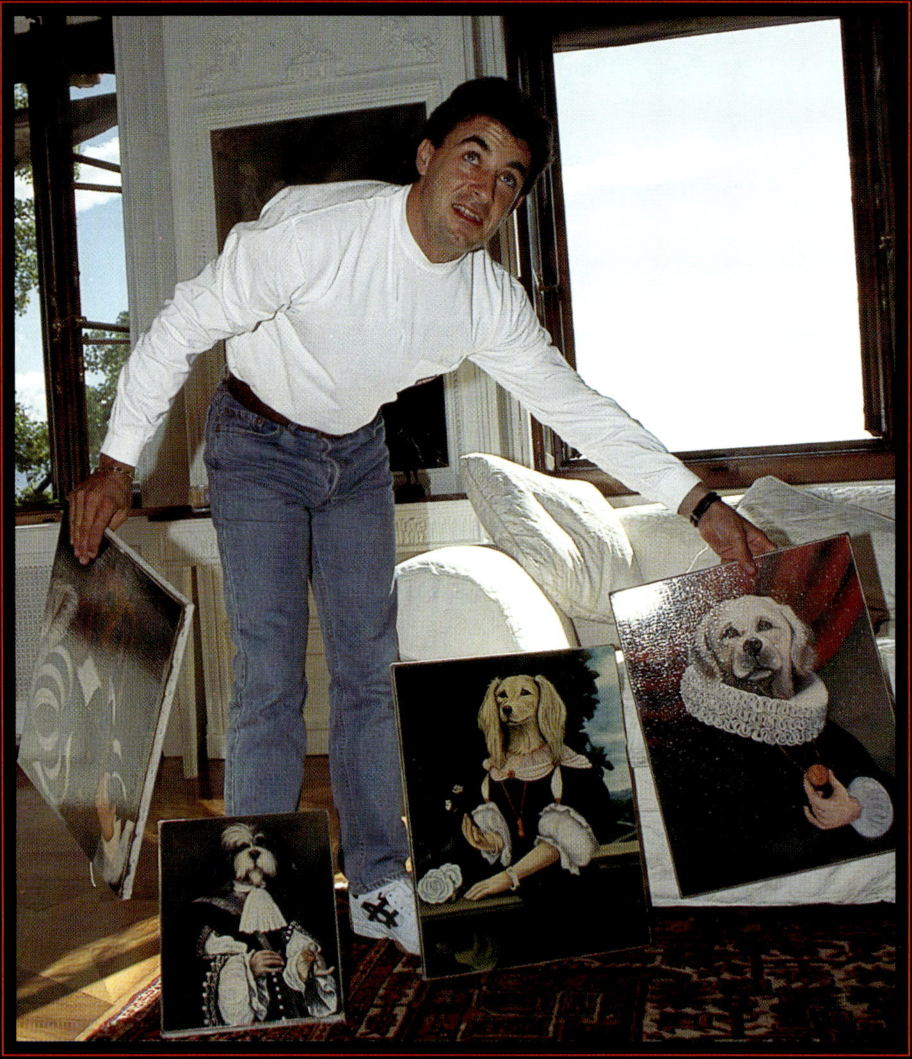

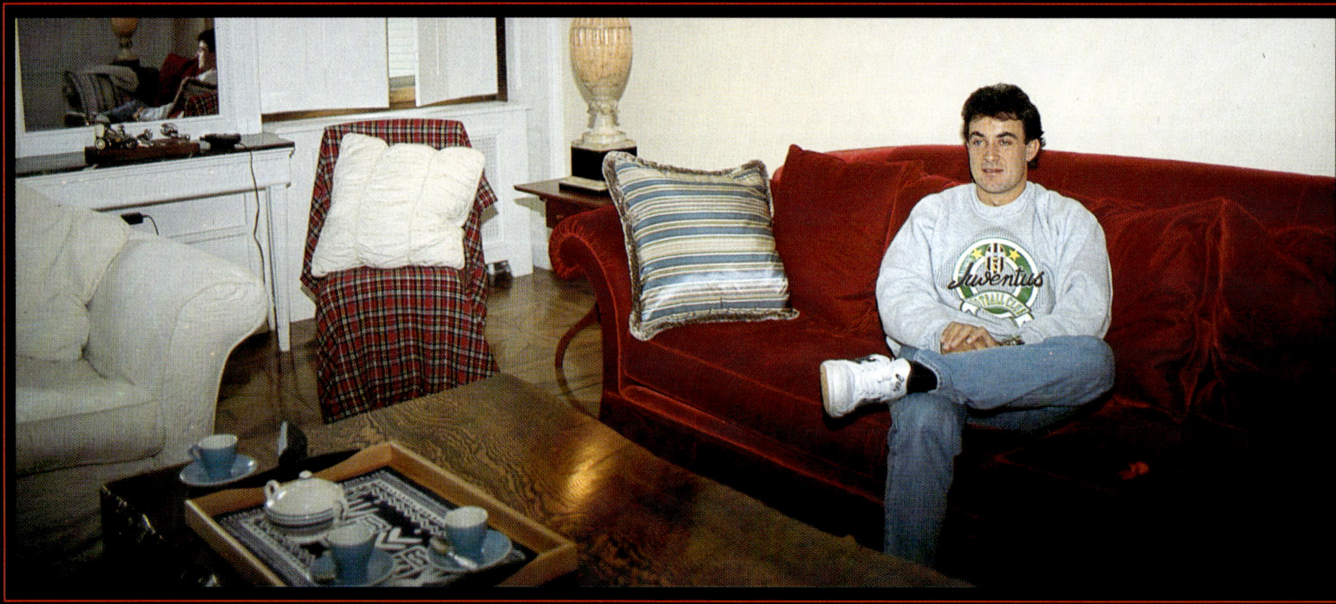
Juventus